W9-AFG-960

To Make a Difference

To Make a DIFFERENCE

A Student Look at America:

Its Values, Its Society and
Its Systems of Education

Edited and with an Introduction by

OTTO BUTZ

HARPER & ROW, PUBLISHERS

New York, Evanston, and London

 For information address Harper & Row, Publishers, Incorporated, 49 East 33rd Street, New York, N.Y. 10016.

LIBRARY OF CONGRESS CATALOG CARD NUMBER: 67-11340

A-S

Contents

Preface

THE essays published in these pages were first given as talks in a student lecture series entitled "To Make a Difference," held on the campus of San Francisco State College in the winter of 1965–66. At the time of writing, the authors were all undergraduate or graduate students at San Francisco State College. The subject to which I asked them to address themselves was their own greatest personal concerns—about themselves, about their society, and about higher education. They were invited to treat the topic from any point of view and with any emphasis they saw fit.

My purpose in arranging the original lectures and in now presenting them in book form has been to contribute to a better understanding of students by Americans generally. I am convinced that the American public has a vital stake in the intellectual and moral ferment being experienced on the campuses of its institutions of higher learning. I believe this to be the case for chiefly two reasons. On the one hand, today's student discontent seems to me to express an enlarged conception of human freedom and an enthusiasm for ideologically uninhibited experimentation of which America at the present juncture of its history stands badly in need. On the other, I see a growing danger that unless young people who are moved by these new attitudes receive at least a sympathetic hearing, more and more of them will give up on the traditional American way of life altogether. Rather than working for its gradual reorientation, they will in one way or another withdraw from it—be it into the country's remaining backwoods, a life of drug experiences, or some form of destructiveness. In my own view, at least, the possibility of such a defection of many of its most gifted and sensitive young people poses a more serious threat to the United States's future than do the much-publicized perils of Communist subversion or attack from abroad.

While contemporary student unrest has been extensively reported in the mass media and analyzed in numerous interpretive studies, the most direct means of probing its dimensions has hardly been tried. That is to give students the opportunity to speak for themselves—not only in the heat of a protest demonstration but in a sustained, reflective way and as much as possible in their own terms.

The difficulty with such firsthand expressions of opinion is, of course, that one can never be sure of their representativeness. How does one know whether the particular person is speaking for anyone but himself? It would, indeed, be possible to avoid this shortcoming by soliciting the views of a statistically representative sample of college students. One could then obtain a reliable picture of the thinking of a whole cross section of today's campus population. Yet this method also suffers from certain limitations. To begin with, it would assume that all those whom one would have to include in a representative sample of our college youth were capable of coherently communicating what they felt and thought. And even if this should be so, it would assume further that it is the sentiments of a cross section of students in which we are most interested. For many purposes this would certainly be true. If, on the other hand, we wish to understand the motivations of the more able of our students who at the same time are registering pressures for cultural change, it obviously is not. In that case we have no alternative but to fall back on more impressionistic criteria, making certain, however, to qualify our findings accordingly.

It is to the latter procedure that I have confined myself in the present project. Some of the student authors I met in the course of my teaching at San Francisco State College; with others I became acquainted in the campus coffee shop. I selected all of them for what seemed to me their greater than average thoughtfulness and without regard to age, sex, family background, political inclinations or academic interests. Since in a statistical sense the essays thus represent only the thinking of their individual authors, they can pretend to be no more than incidental data. It remains for the reader to combine them with such information on the subject as he has gathered from other sources and to evaluate them in the light of whatever tentative conclusions he may already have reached.

For the purposes of this collection I have made several changes from the lecture series as it was first presented. Of the original total of twenty essays I have selected what seemed to me the most interesting ten. And to provide something of a framework and commentary for the essays, I have included a short introduction setting forth a few thoughts of my own. This is not, however, intended as an integral part of the collection itself. It can be skipped over if the reader prefers.

The collection is entirely my own responsibility. It was undertaken without my having informed any officials of San Francisco State College or of the California State College System. All opinions expressed are solely my own or those of the contributing authors. They are in no regard claimed to represent the views of the student body, faculty or administration of San Francisco State College.

In conclusion, I want to express my appreciation to the Associated Students of San Francisco State College for underwriting the cost of taping the lectures, to Fred Kawahara for his conscientious job of recording them, to Marilyn Wollerstein for typing the final draft of the manuscript, and to Dr. Ralph Rust, Claire Salop, Florence Schwartz and Rod Lundquist for their encouragement as the project moved along. I also owe thanks to the Danforth Foundation which, in naming me to one of its Associateships, made available funds with which I was able to defray some of my expenses. I am further indebted to Mrs. Elsa Knight Thompson, Director of Public Affairs at radio station KPFA in Berkeley, for making possible the broadcasting of the original lectures both on KPFA and on its sister station, WBAI in New York. And most deeply of all, I wish to thank the contributing student authors. Without their serious-mindedness and perseverence the entire undertaking would have been impossible. It has been a privilege to get to know them and a pleasure to work with them.

OTTO BUTZ

San Francisco
June 1966

To Make a Difference

Introduction

THE CREATIVENESS OF DISCONTENT

1

IT has long been customary to judge the greatness of nations by the power they are able to bring to bear in international politics. Yet in at least two regards, this is, in fact, an insufficient criterion. For in concerning itself primarily with the external exercise of national power, it diverts attention from the internal circumstances in which that power is rooted and by which its forms of expression are determined. And in using as its referent the extent of a nation's influence over its neighbors, it says nothing at all about the quality of life being experienced within its own borders.

There is another test of national functioning that on human and political grounds is much more meaningful. It is to view the greatness of nations as in the first instance a matter of their ability to satisfy their own citizens. According to this alternative standard, a nation deserves to be called successful in the measure it can keep discontents among its people to a minimum. And it can be considered viable to the extent it is able to accommodate such discontents as arise by making whatever changes are found necessary while still maintaining its historical continuity.

The most obvious advantage of this evaluation of nations is that it assigns a more proper role to the feelings of those most directly involved. Unlike the view suggested by the traditional nation-state ideology, it does not conceive of national collectivities as ends in themselves. It sees them as simply a particular human arrangement, subordinate to the prior human purposes that all such arrangements exist to serve. And while not denying that a people may, indeed, be vitally affected by their nation's power in world affairs, it does not assume that the interests of their nation and their own interests as human beings are necessarily equatable.

But not only does the presence or absence of internal discontents thus offer a more humanly relevant measure of national greatness. It also raises the important question of how nations respond to the discontents they happen to confront. And this, in turn, provides a most significant clue to their political viability. For as history shows, to the extent nations cannot deal with their citizens' internally generated dissatisfactions, they become vulnerable to at least three kinds of crises. They may suffer demoralization and disorganization at home. They may be tempted to evade and project their unresolved internal dissatisfactions through aggressive policies abroad. Or their population may become so disenchanted with the nation as constituted, that they are unable to organize an effective defense when another nation's aggressiveness is directed against them. Unless reversed, each of these eventualities can end in national disaster. Yet in regard to none of them is national greatness in the sense of superior international power of any immediate relevance. The key to all three—to their understanding as well as prevention—lies in the dynamics of a country's internal discontents.

Since our stakes in one another's discontents are so high, it is of utmost importance to keep this index of human feelings under continuous scrutiny. As we look to physical pain as an invaluable clue to disorders in our organic functioning, so it is essential to pay careful attention to expressions of strain and impairment in our larger human dimensions as well. Yet this is not what in fact occurs. Though both pain and discontent serve the same purpose of warning us that something is felt to be wrong, our responses to them sharply differ. Physical pain we treat sympathetically and with a view only to diagnosing the causes of which we assume it to be a symptom. Evidences of hurt engendered by the experiencing of life as a whole we most often react to with hostility and as though they constituted the source of the difficulty in themselves.

The reasons we respond so differently to complaints about our organic functioning and our larger, more specifically human experiences are basically threefold. For one thing, we take it for granted that physical pain is not the sufferer's own fault, and that even if it should be, we are obliged to help him in any ways we can. In regard to expressions of dissatisfactions that go beyond our purely organic condition, this ideal of the Golden Rule and Being One's Brother's Keeper tends to yield to a harsher ethic. That is the morality of the allegedly self-sufficient and competitive individual which underlies so much of our modern Western civilization generally. According to this historically liberal and capitalistic ideology, we are—or should be—the masters of our own psychic, social and economic destinies, deserving credit or blame for whatever may befall us. If, then, we indicate dissatisfactions in these areas of our lives, we seem, in effect, merely to be proclaiming our own failings and seeking to impose on other people.

A second reason for our antipathy toward those who voice discontent involves a defensive reaction intended to protect special privilege. This reaction recognizes that those who express dissatisfactions are demanding some kind of change. And it fears that whatever that change may be, it will jeopardize advantages being enjoyed in the situation that presently exists. It is thus a manifestation of the age-old logic of the haves versus the have nots. And it is bound to operate wherever people live in terms of goods and statuses that must be competed for, either because they actually are in short supply or because the prevailing culture defines them as such.

The final reason we have difficulty in objectively responding to discontents that refer to more than our bodily functioning is the most deep rooted and universal. For it can be a factor even where there is sympathy with those who are expressing dissatisfactions and where no special privileges are being protected. It also stems from a feeling of being threatened. Yet in this case, what is feared is not the loss of any prerogative in itself. The source of the anxiety is the accompanying implied challenge to the personal and social meanings with which the disputed arrangement is felt to be imbued. These meanings have for the most part been built into us since childhood. They serve the essential function of providing our existence with sustaining orientations. And they are never entirely separable from the practices and relationships in terms of which we live. Because of this, any criticism of these familiar circumstances of our lives—that is, of the status quo—is also in some measure an attack upon our meanings. And this, in turn, is experienced as an attack upon ourselves.

While people resist expressions of discontent both because they wish to protect privileges and in order to maintain the integrity of their meanings, it is the latter motivation that engenders by far the greater anxiety. For the fact is that except in regard to the minimal conditions of their survival, human beings do not become emotional in the pursuit or defense of things in themselves. It is true that they often appear to do so, at times to the seemingly irrational point of destroying one another in the process. Yet such apparently irrational behavior is only a matter of our misunderstanding of what they in fact feel is at stake. Their violence is not an expression of their attachment to the disputed phenomena per se (which under different circumstances they might well concede to their opponent without protest). They are anxious because of what the particular objects or practices signify in their scheme of orienting meanings. And if they carry their conflict to destructive extremes, this is only a measure of how crucial they believe these meanings to be.

Those themselves caught up in struggles for and against change are usually unaware how complex their motivations may be. It is therefore impossible simply to ask them about the relative importance of practical and psychological factors in their actions. We can determine this only indirectly. We must infer it from the level of anxieties they display. That is, whenever feelings appear to run high, we can be sure that it is more than any stated particular which is felt to be at issue. The crux of the matter is certain to be some disputed belief which to those involved must remain or become valid if their lives are to have meaning.

Conflicts found to entail what the protagonists perceive as mutually threatening meanings must always be handled from two points of view, the one intellectual, the other psychological. First, they require attention to the divergent beliefs themselves. These must somehow be reconciled—either by reducing them to their more fundamental premises, or by transcending them on some more general level. And second, they require emotional support for the people whose meanings are being revised. For the process of appropriating new beliefs is necessarily an anxiety-inducing experience. In a sense, it amounts to a reshaping of personality. Yet without such simultaneous psychological development, intellectual reorientations alone can accomplish little.

Unfortunately, the intellectual and psychological efforts demanded by such a two-pronged approach are difficult to mobilize. It is therefore usually resorted to only after all else has failed. The more normal responses to demands for change that involve questions of meaning are to suppress or ignore them. Yet both these courses are in the long run self-defeating. To suppress those who challenge existing beliefs is to deal only with symptoms. For all such demands for change are rooted in prior changes in the experiences of those who are expressing them. These, in turn, result from changed circumstances by which the new experiences were formed. And the latter are likely to be so complex and subtle as even to defy being fully comprehended, far less eliminated or reversed.

Nor is it more effective simply to ignore challenges to established meanings. For here again, the changed experiences of which the discontents are an expression remain untouched. It is true that when discontents are ignored they do not assume the extreme forms of hostility that are aroused by policies of suppression. Nevertheless, the possible damages both to the discontented and the rest of the community can be no less ruinous. As has happened with many slighted groups throughout history, the discontented eventually retreat into attitudes of defeat and futility. And sooner or later, increasing numbers of the dominant majority tend to be infected by the same mood. The result is then a weakening of commitments in the entire culture.

Since attempts to suppress and ignore discontents are doomed to failure, there is no practical alternative but to seek to reconcile whatever conflicts of meaning may be involved. Those who realize this and urge that discontents be as fully as possible accommodated thereby mark themselves as true conservatives. For though prepared to subject established values and institutions to change, they know that only by doing so can the community's viability and some version of its traditions be preserved. Those, on the other hand, who reject the logic of continuity through change are in a profound sense radical. For by insisting on the status quo at all cost, they are, in effect, jeopardizing the community's future altogether.

There is a further important reason why expressions of discontent deserve every effort to be understood and accommodated. Not only is such action best suited to maintaining the greatest possible historical continuity; it is also the only alternative compatible with a belief in the dignity of man. It represents a commitment to the notion that the highest good is the most satisfying experiencing of human life. It assumes that the purpose of ideas and institutions is to facilitate this goal as fully as possible. And it trusts each person to decide for himself to what extent it is, in fact, being achieved. It therefore views whatever discontents he may voice not as something to be regretted; it looks upon them as an expression of his most basic right and responsibility as a human being; and it welcomes them as an essential contribution to the practical attainment of the most inclusive possible human self-realization.

Beyond this, openness to expressions of discontent is called for on even more fundamental grounds. For it is the only attitude with the wisdom to accept the inevitableness of change and the humility to recognize that the most we can hope for is to participate in its unfolding. Rather than leading to fear of change, it can thus inspire delight in its continuing creativeness. And rather than inviting vain attempts to obstruct it, it can encourage practical measures to minimize its attendant pains and disruptions.

2

Discontents among members of today's American college generation are directed at four principal targets. Students are demanding an end to all forms of discrimination against Negro Americans. They are pressing for the elimination of poverty and squalor in the society generally. They are sharply critical of United States foreign policies. And many of them are doubtful of the current American way of life in its entirety; they suspect that even when ideally realized, it cannot facilitate a full human existence.

Most immediately, student discontents in these areas are expressed with reference to specific problems and issues. All of them, however, entail fundamental challenges to the values and institutions of American culture as a whole. Indeed, taken together, they add up to a program for change that would require a reorientation of American society to its philosophical and psychological roots.

Student insistence on full acceptance of Negro Americans calls into question Caucasian racial self-consciousness, which has been an integral part of Western civilization for at least a millennium. More specifically, it asks for a redefinition of the historical identity of America itself. It would require abandonment of the United States' self-image as a civilization essentially European. For this would have to be substituted a revitalized notion of the cultural melting pot. And the ideal of this amalgam would have to be extended to include people of all races, and construed to mean unqualified social as well as physical integration.

No less far-reaching challenges to American traditions are implied in student demands for stepped-up attention to social welfare. Not that this ideal is itself alien to the society. The problem, rather, lies in the method of its implementation. As the social history of the past thirty years records, the precondition for progress in these areas has been increasing public expenditures and an ever larger role for government. In practice, these new economic and political directions have been widely accepted. Ideologically speaking, however, they remain largely unassimilated. They have never been reconciled with the persisting notions that the basic allocations of the society's resources ought to be left to the workings of the allegedly free market and that government initiative and planning are essentially undesirable. As a result, all social and economic innovations in the United States have labored under a continuous handicap. If, therefore, governmental responsibility for general levels of welfare were to be expanded to the extent students today urge, this incongruence between ideology and practice would at last have to be confronted. And since it has, in fact, become politically impossible to reverse the trend toward greater initiative by government, the outcome of such a rethinking could not but prove ideologically revolutionary. It would require a drastic revision of economic and political beliefs with which the United States has been identified for most of its history.

Similarly basic conflicts with traditional American thinking underlie student criticisms of United States foreign policies. Like other peoples, Americans have historically subscribed to the notion, "My country, right or wrong." In doing so, they have, in effect, made two assumptions. They have held that the national interest ought to take precedence over universal ethical considerations. And they have believed that such a priority does, in fact, best serve the nation's international power and security. Many of today's students question these assumptions. As a result of the idealization of peace and the self-determination of peoples that marked the United States' participation in World War II, the concern of students for the attainment of these objectives and their sensitivity to their violation have sharply heightened. At the same time, particularly in view of the spread of nuclear weapons, adherence to these standards of international conduct seems to them imperative even on hard political grounds. They therefore believe that the former logic of subordinating ethics to patriotism may no longer be appropriate. They propose instead that a more patriotic expression of patriotism may today be its subordination to an ideal code of universal ethics. Yet since this assumed coincidence of patriotic and ethical considerations cannot always be immediately documented, it leaves them open to easy attack. If pressed, they may feel compelled to admit that they will answer their country's call only if they are convinced that its policies are right. And this, by the older American reasoning, seems tantamount to disloyalty.

The most fundamental student conflict with traditional American meanings concerns their questioning of the American way of life as a whole. Their criticism in this regard is directed at nothing less than the image of man upon which many of the country's most cherished ideals and institutions have been based. They maintain, for example, that the familiar American conception of the individual has been too narrowly preoccupied with freedom of economic enterprise, to the neglect of important other dimensions that human beings innately desire to express. They argue, moreover, that the social competitiveness in terms of which American society compels people to live seriously inhibits them from expressing their own individual uniqueness and sharing their experiences in mutually accepting relationships with others. They also reject most traditional sexual taboos. They prefer, instead, to view sex as inseparable from life as a whole. And they wish—in this matter and generally—to permit each person to live in whatever ways he may find congenial, providing only that he not damage his fellows. They are, in addition, strongly dissatisfied with most popular notions of love. Love, as they understand it, is not something primarily either physical or spiritual; nor is it compatible with any exploitive possessiveness. Ideally, at least, it is viewed as delight in another person's existence, concern for their fullest possible self-realization, and a desire to share with them whatever they may spontaneously wish to share. In these respects and others, today's students are thus engaged in a culturally most original quest. Whereas the entire Judaic-Christian tradition has deeply feared human nature, they wish instead to trust it. And whereas the onus of proof in struggles for human self-expression was formerly on the individual, they wish instead to posit freedom as the norm and to allow its limitation only to the extent such restriction can be demonstrated as truly socially necessary.

Judged in terms of conventional American views of human motivation, the discontents of today's students seems highly paradoxical. As has often been said, these young people belong to the most privileged generation in history. Why, then, can they not simply enjoy their advantages and accept things as they are? Yet such a reaction fails to understand not only what is troubling today's students but also the present situation of the United States as a society. It overlooks the fact that it is precisely those who can look forward to success as their culture defines it who are most naturally inclined to question whether their way of life will bring the human fulfillment it promises. And it does not recognize that it is precisely those who have no further urgent material and social aspirations of their own who are most likely to feel free to evaluate the functioning of their society as a whole.

In a sense, that is to say, present student discontent derives from the very success with which the traditional American dream has to date been implemented. Earlier generations of Americans were necessarily absorbed in making this dream a reality. They therefore felt little occasion to question how satisfying it might prove once it was realized or to empathize with those who might be disadvantaged in the process. They took the validity of American ideals and institutions for granted. And they applied themselves to utilizing them for their own greatest personal gain. Today's young people are at once relatively free from the need for such individualistic economic and social striving and deprived of the consuming sense of purpose it formerly provided. Their identification is with the society as a whole. And they insist that the ideas and functioning of the whole society be meaningful to them. They therefore feel an intense personal concern for greater consistency—between the society's performance and its avowed traditional ideals, and between these traditional ideals and the new needs and possibilities that Americans are today experiencing.

The fact that today's student discontent is as much a product of the successes of American society as it is a reaction to its failings also means that it is unlikely to stop short of its objectives. If these young people sought only some specific economic or social gain, their discontent could be expected to subside as soon as their demand was satisfied. But this is clearly not the case. For one thing, they do not represent any particular disadvantaged group. As college and university students, they come predominantly from the broad American middle class and include representatives of all backgrounds in the American population. And as already indicated, their search for a more meaningful life is at once intensely personal and society-wide in scope. It is in the very nature of their discontents that they cannot be satisfied until American ideas and realities are once again more convincingly brought into line.

The most important task in the interval is to prevent feelings for and against the changes urged by today's students from becoming polarized. The more impatient among the discontented students must be dissuaded from abdicating their commitment to traditional American values and institutions altogether. And those older Americans who feel their traditional meanings most threatened must be convinced that the new needs and opportunities that young people wish to accommodate do, in fact, require recognition.

To sustain a sense of meaningful relatedness among today's students demands a bold rethinking and reorganization of traditional higher education. To prevent the society's disruption by radical conservatives requires a mobilization of the good sense of the entire American people. But if the good sense of Americans is effectively to be brought to bear, they must first be more fully informed as to what the present student discontent most fundamentally entails. They must understand that while it is, indeed, in many ways revolutionary, it is also in a most responsible sense creative. It represents an uncompromising commitment on the part of some of their brightest and most serious-minded offspring to keep America authentic, viable and great.

The New Hero

LOUIS W. CARTWRIGHT*

HOW do I feel about America, her education systems, her institutions, her people, her land, her me? What question could be more important for each of us to answer! Yet how can one sufficiently untangle oneself from the living and struggling of this vast human drama in order to answer it?

It is impossible for me to respond to a subject so consuming and elusive in the stride of a professional. I can't focus on one or two aspects, for I haven't yet become an expert in any one field. Nor, as I see it now, will I in the future specialize in order to be able to say that I know a few things. So, I begin this collection of feelings about America by saying that I don't know anything for sure. I don't think I have ever known anything for sure long enough to remember it. America is that way to me: every now and then I see her for an instant to be a certain country, definable and pin-pointable; but before I get my pen raised to plunge, she disappears in a cloud-twist of change.

Since there is no other proof of one's feelings than living according to them, I'd say mine are healthy. I've lived a quarter of a century and thus far haven't been put away. My wife doesn't run back to Mother and I'm finally through trying to get my father to tell me how to live. I'm punctual and pay my debts, and there is a good chance I'll

* *Louis Cartwright, age twenty-five, is a senior in Psychology. He has worked as a counselor and art teacher with emotionally disturbed and retarded children and plans to set up a school for such youngsters himself. He is also engaged in various creative writing projects.*

instantly like anyone who is and does the same. I'd say I'm doing pretty well. If nothing accidental occurs I might even reach manhood and find out for myself what it's about—providing I can endure the pace I've set for myself, blaming no one else for anything and not seeking salvation tomorrow but always today, now. All this without TV is fairly difficult, but I have faith.

The bomb frightened the daylight out of my life. For two years I didn't make one decision, one plan that bound more than two days together. I continued doing what I had been doing like a castrated bull pacing indifferently among the cows. How many nightmares did I die in? How many mornings did the sun crash into my bed like a surprise party! Finally, out of a desperation to live, I decided that the bomb didn't matter, that if it came today we wouldn't have to face dying the day after. I might as well make big plans, seeing as how nothing had changed. So I made big plans and still make them. But like hell it hasn't changed! I'm probably more religious now than the most devout Jehovah's Witness, but I have no one to pray to. I am devoted to life, health and future, to preserve these in the nowness of every thought, wish and dream. The only one left to believe in is Man, so I figure we've got to prepare him for the responsibilities of being God. And we've got to start with ourselves. Which means we have to start all over again, look at it all as if we had just arrived like children walking to school for the first time. To these ends, then, my life is a first attempt and my feelings are my only guide.

I trust myself at the intuitive level. Propaganda may be pulling me here and there, and it may not be; I don't know. I don't deal decisions out to distant realities like Vietnam. All I know is I don't have any reasons to kill anyone, and I'm the one who has to have them in order to do it. I can't be pushed or bullied into a war I don't understand. That goes for all things of that nature. The term civil rights means nothing to me, but a person getting unfairly shafted means everything. I'll just have to say I don't have time for sit-ins and marches; I'm too busy learning how to live. Besides, most sit-ins and marches are too popular to be effective; in a sense they've been wasted on too many little points. However, they might be the only method of resistance against the State for those of us who can't afford a lobby. I might be wrong not to march or sit, but I just haven't felt it yet. I might be committing huge mistakes that in two years will rise up and hurl a shadow over my life, force me into that corner from which the only escape is to the analyst or Mr. Tambourine Man. There are so many might-be's in my style of life, too many to waste my time in elaborate and absolute preparation. So I keep open to the front and worry only about my back.

I am not contemporary, popular, in the "new look" of the "Pepsi Generation," and I'm not frightened. This party has been going on so long now, that I think if someone announced that it was over nobody would leave. They'd have no place to go. I get the same feeling when I pass a bar at two o'clock and listen to the homeless begging not to be thrown out. If television were suddenly canceled what would people do? All that free time? Occasionally I feel trapped by the outstanding accomplishments of the Beatles, the overnight success of skateboards and hula hoops . . . I find myself trying to come up with a gimmick to make a million. Then I wake up and grab myself by the collar: What? You want to create another ride for them to spend their time on? Then I begin to blame these heroes who throw the people a bone for their money and model nothing but materialism to our children. But, hell, it isn't them. It's the potential in the situation that pays their type, and the situation has never been anything but a blueprint unraveling; it's we who create the morality from it; by morality I mean the way to be, and the way to be is to choose your hero and dress him in money, and it is still of the people. I guess I'm just lonely believing I got my morality from the Earth: the animal in me and at large is in stride with a higher truth than my intellect can handle. Morality is the intellect's attempt to protect itself against the animal, but it is only an aftereffect of life and the animal knows this. We Americans have always fought the animal by ignoring it. Our morality has been a blindfold to wear in the daytime and a sleeping pill to take at night. I've experimented at living without masks and pills and, no kidding, it's all right. We're pretty damn fine animals when we loosen up the cinch and remove the bit.

It's all a matter of fads and trends, of the short-run and the long-run, of the eternal trend of mankind; the rest is the Fourth of July and firecrackers, and anybody knows where to buy them. So you pop 'em off; I don't care.

America has seldom been more than a list of many moving spirits clashing, joining, splitting, some small and violent, others huge and bullying, but it has never been describable in terms of one spirit. (Although the Beatles might take some issue.) Today I see a spirit moving in America almost as widespread as the heavy silence following Kennedy's assassination; this is the spirit of uniformity. It seems to bulldoze everything unique and human down until the ground is flat enough for one hundred square miles of identical houses. And I don't have to wait for history to come along with its approval or condemnaton of my opinion; I am the pen-point of history writing, my life is its ink. I am defining myself en route, knowing that before the ink is dry what I've written is already inaccurate, for I am a process of becoming different. And this gives me hope.

I am a rear-engine sports car, a Lotus or a Porsche pushing myself into the future of blind curves and diminishing left-handers. I am prepared for the unexpected, I lunge toward it with hunger, even though I've seen so much I seldom encounter a surprise; however, I am most near death when I begin believing I've seen it all. So I continuously doubt the future. My faith is behind me, not out in front: I am not drawn ahead by the apron strings of Heaven; I am pushing at crashing speeds into the unknowns, whether or not I interrupt any heavens. I've made no contract with God; his promises and threats do not interest or frighten me. A life after death is not separated by dying: I die into dream each night and am sifted or jolted back into life each morning. My power is in me, in all of us. Life is this power.

Self-reliance or -directedness is the first inevitable step out of alienation and solitude, and since solitude is such a shocking realization it leaves a scar or flaw in our subsequent adjustment to life. I call this scar a sense of privacy. You might look on it as a void in one's personality which he fills with his very own ideas of the universe; in here he writes philosophy for himself and his dependents. Here, then, is the factory of self-reliance. Others might look upon this void or room as a guest cottage for God, a place we go to pray, an island of insanity. Indirectly self-reliance is manufactured there no matter what you call it.

The obvious counterpart or concomitant of being self-directed is that I profoundly resent anyone interfering by ordering me to do something or go somewhere. Once my father directed my life; when I left home I took over; on occasion he will ask me to do something for him, but it is no longer an order and he has heard my refusal. The police and the selective service don't respect me and my sense of privacy. This is a real fact, and I know it, so it is again up to me to stay out of their way if I want to remain in charge of my doings. Needless to say, I have been negligent and have put myself in positions where they pushed me. You see, I keep forgetting that they no longer keep the peace; they enforce law and so disturb peace. I forget that they do not deal with humans as being human; they deal with humans as being lawbreakers. I forget that one cannot be innocent or ignorant or have lapses into innocence because those states of being are illegal. I guess I forget because I want to. I don't want to recall that I grew up in a town where I was ordered to show a policeman my identification card three or four times a week. There's no excuse for me forgetting that! I should not take walks at night; I know better.

Also, I loathe the notion America is promoting that one has to go to college in order to "make it." How about those who don't want to? Those who have a couple of dreams of their own that they'd like to try out? When a notion like that becomes almost an unwritten law, a matter of course, then we defeat ourselves: we end up forcing pure character and imagination, our only chance for health and future, into systems of education that return to us a beast who is intelligent only because he has finally been trained to answer with the acceptable notions of our time. Once so potentially brilliant and eager to learn about life, they return to us predictably dull and bored under the oppressive weight of collections of information. We frustrate the creative mind into a desperate submission whereupon it closes up like a clam on the ocean floor and never feels good or free about life again. Some of our young blood isn't meant for college even though it can pass the entrance exams, but where else are they encouraged to go? Into the Army? The parent offers to send him to, and support him through, college only if he goes directly after high school and stays with it for a continuous four years (or is it six, now?). So they go, are never late, are never passionate, sit in classrooms, while the life they felt to be good quietly dies.

I first enrolled in college because I wanted to. This was two years after high school, after I had hitchhiked around America, after having cycled a year in Europe, and worked in a missile factory—after, I'd like to say, I felt that I had earned the readiness for learning. I wanted to learn all about the Greeks, especially Odysseus, for he, like me, had traveled. But I wasn't allowed to take Greek Mythology or study the Greek language; I had to take certain *preliminary* courses. I did manage to lie my way into a philosophy class. At the end of that year I felt that I had had enough; I knew that I could learn without having an examination date placed before me for discipline. I still liked learning. So I quit and returned to Europe. My father was astounded and hurt at my courteous refusal of the security of a college degree; he made me feel like I was cheating. But he wished me good luck and a quick return.

My first trip to Europe had been a magic carpet tour; I had enough money, and though I cycled I didn't need to work my way, didn't need to stay any place longer than it pleased me. The second trip was the yes-trip: it was yes to everything, and I was broke. I took jobs doing anything, lived anywhere, ate anything, and learned a great deal about freedom. For instance, I learned that you can cycle all day in the rain and not catch cold if you work hard (and if your clothes get washed). I didn't belong in school, anyone could see that. I needed to try myself in life, see if I could learn how to be. From where I was in the south of France, American middle-class security looked like a sickness, one that most never got over. When I returned home, in spite of the particular mood I was in or my reason for returning, I was full of life and lean as a coyote. I wanted to sleep, then eat, then think.

"But he's got to finish college," I heard my father saying to my mother behind their door that night.

"Let him rest awhile," said mother.

"Hell, rest, he's twenty-one. When I was his age I was supporting my parents."

"We don't need support."

"I don't want his support, I want him to get to work. It's not healthy to sit and do nothing."

I listened to them. My father was right. So was I. He wouldn't give in and neither would I. The last favor I wanted of my parents was time, time to decide what I wanted to try next. Three months later I introduced him to my fiancée, and within a month, married, I left that time and place of my childhood forever.

A year later I wanted to return to school to pursue a new interest, and within a week I hated college. It was stuffy, crowded, tightly scheduled, fast, an authority center where questions were slaughtered quickly and efficiently with brilliant little answers. I had to put away my interests and get in line with the others. It wasn't learning; it was read, memorize and answer, and there wasn't any time for exceptions to the beautiful rules. It was terrible, but I had unwittingly promised myself that I would stick it out. I'd convinced myself that like climbing a long, steep grade, there is a personal benefit gained in reaching the top. So here fulfilling my promise was my only reason for remaining. Endurance.

My reason for enduring became a chant I whisper to myself when it gets worse than bad: you can make it, you made it over the Alps, you can do anything. Don't I have other reasons? Would I come to watch people? I'd rather stand on Market Street.[1] Would I come to learn from teachers? We all know how unnecessary and redundant many professors are, how they never quite come alive before their classes, as if the administration were controlling their oxygen supply. Most classrooms are holding a recital of the text you read last night. But every now and then, one man sneaks through and holds a class on his own that balances off the entire history of inadequate professors. Yes, for that chance (as long as it doesn't get any slimmer) I'd sign up for a full load and attend. But isn't it so very unfortunate that the clothesline of education droops so low between the occasional giants? To this point I append the twin to the statement that all of us shouldn't go to college: all of those who are teaching shouldn't be. Perhaps half of all who populate a campus should be in a trade school or on a ranch. I feel we have sacrificed learning for education, that, as with missiles, we are competing with Russia to graduate people, hit or miss. No! No no no no. We fail beneath the statistical affidavits of our success: there it is in black and white, but there it ain't in the people.

[1] San Francisco's main business and shopping thoroughfare, running from the Ferry Building to Twin Peaks.

Another aspect of this swelling horror is the soul-shrinking speed at which we educate! Got to hurry, got to meet my future in four years, go go—college à go-go. I imagine an IBM computer graduating twenty thousand cards and there's no one there to claim them. What's the hurry? It reminds me of the Yiddish saying: *Sleep fast, we need the pillows.* Along with this preoccupation with speed develops the feeling that one is supposed to know a few things simply because he is nearing the exit. The poor beast, he knows all the right answers in his field and he is secure. Meantime, as Bob Dylan sings in one of his verses, life goes on all about him.

Nope. Our country wants our colleges to do more than they can honestly do, so it forces them to be dishonest. Do anything you have to do but make sure the statistics are ready in time to be published in the July 1 issue of *Time*. One million graduate this June!

I'm in no hurry and resent being shoved. A college or university should be slow and easy. It shouldn't have too clear of an idea what an educated man should know. There should be no such system as a major and a minor and so many of each kind of units to sign up for. Curiosity if left alone will fill out a healthy program. And professors should be paid enough to keep them from griping about salaries in the classroom. They sometimes remind me of the street performer who has to send his hat about the crowd.

College should be a free place with huge doors that swing open to whomever feels curious about what goes on inside. It shouldn't be a prerequisite to life; it is an aftereffect. I've learned and have been inspired more by my time spent in coffee bars and cafeterias with others than in the hours I've sat in classrooms. But I get no credit for that time. So maybe classes should be held in the college cafeteria. I want it to be that free and slow. The way I describe how a college should be, it becomes obvious that we have very few colleges in America. We have trade schools where one learns how to do psychology and engineering and creative writing, and where curiosity is called game playing and inefficient. After all, if you keep asking those questions, you'll never get out by June!

The university is not an ivory tower without a city to be ivory for; they are inseparable. But America separates them. The American student is in constant conflict between working to earn enough to go to school and studying to earn the grades to stay in school. And most often he can't get a job in the field of his studies. So combine work with school. Give him not only a salary but college credit for his time spent on the job, for isn't experience the best way to learn? The new work-study program sponsored by the government is a timid step in this direction. But it still doesn't reacquaint the city with the college, and this is essential.

America devises or chooses so many easy ways out. College is now an easy way out of worrying about becoming a success. You get a degree and they've got it all worked out for you on an easy-to-understand form which lists how long it will take to be earning twenty-five thousand a year. And this goes for all the other easy ways out.

Some afternoons a few of us would gather for coffee in the cafeteria and discuss our private lives and their progress toward freedom. One would describe his latest LSD trip, another would remind us that marijuana is still a good ride, and someone from another state would say, "Yeah, those are good but haven't you tried mushrooms or cactus?" On and on it would go. I was always the one who after a few rounds began to tell about my latest fishing or hunting trip. I would try to describe it vividly so as to remind them that life is still a pretty good trip. I would "trip out" discussing my trip (they called it "zooming," which means getting carried away). They often wondered what I was taking. After my story I tried to convince them that they didn't need pills to be free, that LSD is most often a pause, time out from facing reality as it will be when they return. However, there were always more of them than me, so I would lose, so to speak, to someone else's LSD vacation story. Oo! The colors! On those days I left school feeling so very lonely I didn't see why or how I could return.

If you take the pill, then chemically you are *forced* to look *freely* at yourself. It is as if we no longer have it within ourselves to reach out and touch the terrible truths, as if we haven't the faith and guts to get us there on our own. Where is America's confidence? The confidence that doesn't depend on pills and degrees and sunglasses, on the new look and the club card, and approval of the authority. Have our governments and schools done so much for us that we have completely forgotten that we can do some things on our own? Why do the majority of professors have to write out a lecture to read to their class? What happened to "off-the-cuff"?

Maybe it is my fault for not being able to see that we have reached a new level of life where only institutions can handle humanity and where the individual is the element of error that must be canceled out. If that is it then I don't want it. Progress can carry America wherever she wants to go, but I'm glad my feet are on the earth and I enjoy walking.

Whose America *is* this? I no longer feel a part of her. I am a stranger in her schools and indifferent to, or against, her goals (or the possible lack thereof). I've pulled my car off the circuit, quit the race to nowhere; now I drive where I want to, and it is up to me to keep out of her way if I want to keep free. (Isn't that ironic? I have to fight America for my freedom!)

My America is me alive and living, wading upstream, crashing through brush, chasing grunion, watching salmon leap, screeching my brakes on the freeway to watch a flight of Canadian geese, picking up a hitchhiker and asking him where he's going, having coffee with a trucker, finding an arrowhead, and being attacked by a blackbird because I passed too near her nest. America is me getting up tired and driving thirty miles to meet someone on time, or hiking up mountains just to do it. It's the whole country when you look around from a mountain fourteen thousand feet tall. It's feeling as if fences are merely spider webs that cling to your pants legs when you go roaming. It isn't a job at ten thousand a year, a club to drink in, a fast red car, and a pasteboard house; and it isn't going to be that ulcer at forty, either. Sometimes I think *I'm* America.

America: a big place, fragmented by rules into smaller places, further broken up by borders into smaller places, and finally, unfindable on a country map, my town, a peephole through which I interact with and spy on the world—if and when I choose to. If I choose not to, they will try to force me to, and though it would take sixty days for Washington's red paper snake to strike me into her army, I'd rather make them use it than submit like a good son. I'm no son of Washington.

Yep! America's a big place, but it barely has room for me. I live on its borders, up against its cultural limits at all times. The cost of living on the border is high: you've got to be wealthy, and wealth here is measured in terms of how little you need to live. How few possessions. I need so little I have to make up reasons for not retiring tomorrow. I'm lean. I'm a tramp playing dress-up. My possessions are souvenirs, they are not necessaries. I do not need the luxuries this country uses to bait its people toward progress. I've learned to despise that word.

For whenever we look about to see what it was we were working for, what do we see: a house that wasn't built well enough to raise our children, broken appliances in the garage, two cars falling apart while only one or two years old, furniture that was once so pretty you felt you had to cover it with plastic, an electric kitchen with a trash box full of TV dinner tins. Is this the only other way to avoid another crash: to build stuff so cheaply it will break down and have to be bought again and again? The other way to keep this economy going is to keep a war going. Is this all to build a home for the brave to preserve freedom? No, I'm afraid no one will buy that one any more. We all know that we don't know why we're doing all the things we do, that we don't like what we do, but we don't know what to do about it. Okay, it is easy to say what is happening, and it is easy to list a few reasons why. But what to do about it? What do we do?

It would be pointless to list ways we could alter this situation unless I thought we would do it, and that is the sorrow that weighs me down: I don't think most Americans want to change; they have faith in these systems. Oh, they might argue this in the bar after work with their friends when it doesn't count, but be sure that the next morning they'll be back at the bench performing some push-button task that in some way supports the sicknesses of our time. Whether it's throwing together pasteboard houses, squeezing food into heat-and-serve tins, printing stories they know are just half-true, creating advertising to further confuse and take advantage of others like themselves who no longer know better. Each one plays a small-enough role so he doesn't feel accountable. It's *they* who are doing it, the owners, the board, the office. "Don't look at me, buddy, I just work here."

The other night my wife and I went to a drive-in movie. At the intermission I went in to get her an ice water and a coffee. I poured myself the coffee and asked the girl to please fix me an ice water. She turned to the boy cashier: "How much do we have to charge for the large cup?"

He didn't turn his head: "Twenty-five cents," he answered.

I couldn't believe I heard him right. "No," I said, "it's just a cup of ice water."

He turned smilingly: "I know, but it doesn't matter. The cups are on inventory. Everyone that goes out of here I have to get twenty-five cents for."

"Look," I said, "the cup probably cost three cents at best. How can you charge a quarter for it? I don't care about inventory."

"But the office made the inventory. It's a rule."

"Well, break the damn rule! It's ridiculous."

"How do I explain it to them? There's supposed to be a quarter for each cup."

"Tell them you stepped on one."

"Nah, I couldn't do that."

"Aren't you part of them?" I asked.

"No, I just work here."

"Oh, you're their slave, then?"

"What do you mean?" he asked.

"You are part of this company. All you'd have to do is leave a note for the inventory saying you sold one cup for a nickel."

"I can't do it, I'm sorry."

"Because of them?"

"Yes."

"You know, friend, you're dead. I don't know why anyone would ever want to talk to you. I couldn't stand behind a counter if I had to point blame to my "they" every time something different came up. Don't you realize that every time you shirk and shrug off responsibility you make yourself smaller? You've already shrunk to a pip-squeak."

He just smiled at me like a baby who thinks it's funny to see anger. So did all the people crowding around, but no one said anything or got too close. They wouldn't have done anything to stop me from killing the dead-boy.

"Look," I said with great tolerance, "I'll give you one more chance. You sell me the cup for twenty-five cents. I'll bring it back, wash it, and you give me twenty cents return on it, okay?"

"I can't do it. How would I explain the five cents extra in the drawer?"

"PUT IT IN YOUR POCKET!"

The speechless dead-boy stood expressionless, like he didn't understand a word I had said. I held his eyes sternly as I strode out of the refreshment room. No one said a word. They didn't even call me a nut behind my back. On the way back to the car I counted four empty cups blowing around in the wind.

I know that these kinds of Americans, the ones you'll never hear about unless they get killed in a spectacular accident, are not strong enough to begin a battle back to reality, to that state of knowing you are alone and that each person has his own idea of himself and you, and that beyond this we know nothing for sure. It is a state of dignity and responsibility to eternity which includes this moment. Some try to return to this state of awareness; they sink in despair at the odds with which they're faced. Others don't try; they sink silently into systems they don't understand. A few make it. They are put into institutions for safekeeping. But the dead-boy behind the counter sits safely inside a stockade made up of fears he doesn't look at. If he steps out in any direction he's afraid he'll be attacked. He's a nobody and an anybody. So what'll happen to him? Who'll help him? No one. So stay there and blame them, blame the boss who isn't here right now. So, each of us lives on that pinhead surrounded by others like ourselves who will point at us if we move. That doesn't stop some from moving but it stops most.

Therefore we needn't be surprised when we read that a woman was raped in a New York building in front of many witnesses, or that a man was killed in front of the same. It's the law that you are not supposed to interfere with the scene of an accident. So better drive by and be glad it wasn't you who careened off that embankment and are now crying in pain wishing some fragmented person like yourself would break the law and stop to help you. When the people of a country won't or can't help one another then it is no longer a country.

We won't help one another but we are herded off in battalions to help Vietnam! America, the big meat producer, has something wrong with her and she blames others for the whyness of the war that she needs to fight in order to keep her sick economy flowing. Why are the best of our youths devising huge gambles in order not to be drafted? Faking homosexuality, psychoses, and nervous breakdowns, or flatly refusing to go and thereby putting themselves in jail. They are doing this because they believe there is no longer any cause great enough to kill others for. They have become responsible to humanity, for all wars now have a red line, a point beyond which we cannot go and survive. In this respect the bomb is a blessing, for it gives us an unarguable reason not to try to prove our points in other countries, spilling blood of people who never heard of America.

When I think of war, of bombs startling children and splashing horror on faces of screaming mothers I nearly go mad with anger! While I'm sitting in the cafeteria having coffee or on a stream at dawn feeling very happy, all of a sudden the image of war goose-steps into my mind and I scream: Why? What for? Who for? A million pettinesses crawl quickly like ants to answer those questions. I know it isn't just America, that there have to be at least two to have a war, that the innocent always get it, and that others make money on it, and that others die in it, and that some don't care a damn about it. Okay, this is reality and I know it, but I'm not relieved of anger. I want to fight something, whatever it is, that creates war. But when I try to express my feelings someone nails me down to the hard facts of life as if these facts were the sacred Part Two of the Ten Commandments. I want to fight these facts.

When I fight I am like all neurotics who have waged a war alone. I have no one to compare myself to, no one out there to keep me honest, no one to tell me to go home when my opposition has disappeared. Often I feel like the kid who gets mad when a bunch of his friends playfully pile on top of him. The madness builds up as their laughter loudens, until it cannot be contained, and the boy explodes with unconquerable strength; he breaks loose and swings. He slugs everyone standing around. And he can't stop himself. America sometimes feels like a hundred bags labeled friendship being piled on top of me; I tear loose and rip them all open just to see them pour out. Of course I don't trust everyone. I trust about ten people, and I trust them to be just who they are, not me. But I don't trust

America. It thinks friendship can be won during a party, or at least let's all forget about it and have a good time together. Well, that's it, I can't forget. I can't forget that America doesn't want to mean what it says, that it isn't fighting for freedom, that we are not the great home of the brave. And I can't forget that it is my fault, for the others do not care. I miss the America I dreamt about.

When I, the People, learn to remember, when I the People, use the lessons of yesterday and no longer forget who robbed me last year, who played me for a fool—then there will be no speaker in all the world to say the name: "The People," with any fleck of a sneer in his voice or any far-off smile of derision.[2]

* * * *

I guess having been banged around by those bags of false friendship has made me sound pretty strong and angry. I even surprised myself. I said that I blame myself for everything and turned right around and began blaming others for not remembering, not having the strength to keep reality in focus long enough to become reacquainted with it. I must now state that I haven't written one sentence against America that was not first composed in self-disgust. At one time or another I, too, forgot about everything painful or challenging. I, too, used the word love as only a technique for snowing a girl into bed. I, too, passed the blame to the *They* of America. I didn't know any better. Oh, I felt different, but feelings aren't necessarily expedient. "You can't get anywhere being honest, Mac." The worst most unhealthy person I see today I wouldn't be able to understand unless I had at one time stood in his shoes. I recognize those shoes. I used to be very sick, and that was when I was considered by my elders to be most healthy. Now I am well and clean, and they consider me to be sick. There is not merely a matter of opinion, either.

Every time I kept quiet, put off something I felt for fear of endangering my standing in a group, I began to hate myself. This hate would build up, collect in some recess of my personality, until I was

[2] From "I Am the People, the Mob," from *Chicago Poems* by Carl Sandburg. Copyright 1916 by Holt, Rinehart and Winston, Inc. Copyright 1944 by Carl Sandburg. Reprinted by permission of Holt, Rinehart and Winston, Inc.

so divided against myself I would have to break open. If I was right I had to argue and fight. If I was wrong and knew it, I had to break down my old feelings and sweat it out forming new ones that were still strange to me. After about fifteen years of this I have finally learned not to keep quiet, not to postpone, not to let someone else do it for fear of getting myself involved too deeply. I don't want to keep quiet any more, and I won't forget anything to make being noisy easier.

Let me backtrack a moment to pick up the points I've tried to make. First, I don't feel a part of America any more: I don't believe in her reasons; I don't learn from her schools; and her systems and laws have just about controlled the human element out of the experiment. Second, I can't forget the fullness of the world in order to make my life easier. Third, I have promised myself not to keep quiet any longer, for I feel to blame for everything, which makes me responsible. And fourth, I can't be pushed into a war or way of life I don't feel to be true. Death would be sweeter than a deadly lifetime, and I feel that is the goal of American progress, which leaves me out.

Why do I feel to blame?

It is simple: I am not part of the system, and the system's hopes, ends and means, but I am part of the people. I am responsible to them and the land. I am responsible to that part in each that each has forgotten, the dark side of their personalities' moon, their subconscious, their back-forgotten. I get along best with those of us we've locked up because we think we can't get along with them. The ones who can't hide any more because they have no place left to run to, the juvenile delinquents, the drunks, neurotics still at large, and other yet unclassified people who are trying to do what they want to do without causing too much of a disturbance. When I say "the people" I refer to those who still try to enrich their lives by seeking out reality, not evading it. The others who coast along from ride to ride with a pocketful of free passes are the dead weight who have to be awakened to the fact that they are being carried.

There are none living in America today who are more lonesome than the responsible. These are people who have made it their primary goal to form a functional overview of mankind and live within and nourish this view. I don't know who said so, or even if it has been announced yet, but every man has a duty to develop a philosophy that he would rule the world by if he were elected king. In a small way every father does this if he's worth a damn. Unfortunately for most of the children born since World War II, this duty has been sorrowfully neglected, purposively forgotten, ignored.

Bobby Dylan sings in one of his verses, that he hasn't anything to live for. I did. My father was a big, warm man, active and responsible, and he truly loved his sons. In the old style to some, in just plain style to me, he could make me believe there were fish in rain puddles. I had to live a long way up to reach and befriend him on that highest of all friendship planes—father and son. I felt it my duty to learn all that he knew. He was there. Behind him stood my mother.

Now he is not there (in the same way). Behind him stand the mountains. He now stands in me and I still have someone to live up to: myself.

Looking around I can find nothing that we need more than men who will fulfill the duty of king. We need fathers. We've plenty of mothers, too much mama. What does Dylan mean when he says: "I've got no one to live up to." He's saying this, in the song, to his mother. He's saying there's nobody he respects more than himself, that he doesn't have any idea of a better man, no hero, nobody he would pattern his life after. I believe a boy needs this. He needs to see what becoming a man means, the same way a girl needs to see what mothering means. Children need models to aim their lives toward. Without them society stops growing, codes fall apart, lives begin to be lived from day to day and fad to fad, planning spans shorten, hopes shrink, discipline loses its value, nobility vanishes—all life loses its ability to endure.

I have an egocentric view of the universe; I know that man is the center no matter where he is. The father is the center of the family. He is a guide. He takes his son on trips into the world. He answers unanswerable questions by simply saying: "I don't know." He earns his son's respect by being respectable. In short, the father is there like the mother is there, and he doesn't close the door when he feels like screaming at God. He encourages strength and guts by being strong and persevering. He models his own image of man to his son. When the son grows strong enough to leave, the father is still there to model dignity of age. This is the greatest gift a father can give his son: the image of a strong, warm man. And a father can't give it if he doesn't have it, and he can't get it without learning what it means to be a man.

In all strong nations the father has been there in the center along with a strong mother—in rich balance. He is not in American culture today. He was once upon a time. The old heroes that haunt our deepest dreams and who confuse our decisions as to how and what to try for in our lives come from this era of America: the pioneer, the broad-minded Irish-American priest, the Gary Coopers of all the High Noons of life who face their enemies in the open, the individual politician who wouldn't be bought, the Elmer Gantrys who stumble pugnaciously into true religion—these heroes still walk tall through our dreams, but they're seldom encountered on the street, at work, at church, and on the speaker's platform. So we miss them. This is what I meant when I said that this is not the America I dreamt about.

I also said I didn't think that most Americans were strong enough to begin to walk back to the world—as it is. They don't have the guts to be that responsible, and they don't have it because they don't believe it is necessary in order for them to get along. But what about their children? I'm sure a man can sneak through life without getting touched, but I don't think that man's child can. We need models of the best make, models that reflect universes of possibility. We don't have them.

William Butler Yeats's poem *The Second Coming* paints the picture I'm trying to get at so vividly that I cite it here in full:

> Turning and turning in the widening gyre
> The falcon cannot hear the falconer;
> Things fall apart; the centre cannot hold;
> Mere anarchy is loosed upon the world,
> The blood-dimmed tide is loosed, and everywhere
> The ceremony of innocence is drowned;
> The best lack all conviction, while the worst
> Are full of passionate intensity.

Surely some revelation is at hand;
Surely the Second Coming is at hand.
The Second Coming! Hardly are those words out
When a vast image out of *Spiritus Mundi*
Troubles my sight: somewhere in sands of the desert
A shape with lion body and the head of a man,
A gaze blank and pitiless as the sun,
Is moving its slow thighs, while all about it
Reel shadows of the indignant desert birds.
The darkness drops again; but now I know
That twenty centuries of stony sleep
Were vexed to nightmare by a rocking cradle
And what rough beast, its hour come round at last,
Slouches towards Bethlehem to be born?[3]

America is big, so big a man doesn't know how to be any more. He doesn't know how to raise his children to be, either. Because he no longer knows what his country is. He, like the falcon, cannot hear it call to him to come this way or go that way. Truly, the center of America cannot hold us together, for no two of us know the same center. Therefore there is no center. Just as cities break up into shopping centers, our government has disassembled into bureaus in which no one man is responsible or accountable for anything—all is left up to the committee that is going to meet as soon as it has been formed. Which means that the only responsible item left is the system. This is America.

It is vague, big, impersonal, undefined, soft, sloppy. America is a slob. A thing that collects unemployment pay whenever it gets the chance. No one has to be true to anything: the system will take care of who is honest and who is not. The system is sick, and the people are without courage. The best have no confidence and the worst have too much.

But we still have a chance; all our seeds aren't bad. The few old hero-types who are left will be coming out more and more; they always do when things get bad. As a band of animals drives off the one of them that is sick, so these Americans will drive sick America

[3] Reprinted with permission of The Macmillan Company from *Later Poems* by William Butler Yeats. Copyright The Macmillan Company 1924, renewed 1952 by Bertha Georgie Yeats.

out of business. They will beg for responsible positions and then gamble them against the truth and health of every little incident with which they have to deal. Professors who refuse to be bullied by administrators, personnel managers who refuse to be blinded by the degree, men who still search for personal character and strength—anyplace you find a person living by principles that grow in scope as he learns you find what I call an American. And yes, he looks primitive and ridiculous standing out there all alone. He is an old hero. And he will die nobly. But the others, the faceless gray murmur in every crowd, will need an expensive funeral, for contrast, so that their mourners will think that they had lived.

And where are the new heroes? Who are they? How do they live? Are they slouching beneath the shadows of the indignant dying American majority toward some Bethlehem to be born? Has Man been asleep for twenty centuries because he believed that Christ paid the price of wakefulness and that this price could be paid just once by one and not always by all? Then, what weird hero-child carries the nightmare of this two thousand years in his innocent and willing head?

When I ask, Who is the new hero? I'm not looking for a name, a celebrity, any one person. I'm looking for the image we have of our own best self. The new hero is one who is following after this image, but, unlike the donkey that follows after the farmer's carrot, he holds his own carrot out in front, and this keeps him honest. I'm not going to say that Zorba[4] is the hero, or that Bobby Dylan is the hero; but I would say that they and others have by example added to the portrait of a potential hero. You could say that potential is the hero, potential wherever it is found and expressed.

So I say the new hero is a world personality, for we are a potential world of men who require no corrals, who seek and enjoy freedom of being at ease among ourselves. If we can dream of a united world we can have one. All dreams are mirages of realities just beyond our present reach; tomorrow they will have a snow-cone stand in the middle of the Sahara!

He's new, not yet standing, "moving his slow thighs," but he's

[4] Nikos Kazantzakis, *Zorba the Greek,* New York, Simon and Schuster, 1952. Also the film by the same name.

here. He's a rough beast to handle because he can't think in terms of discriminant groups, nations, cultures; he thinks in terms of *Man.* Patriotism is a part of the two-thousand-year-old nightmare he has; the definition of the word stymies him, for he has no feeling with which to fuel it. He's like the country boy who's gone to the city and now can't stand his small town, can't take a job in his father's firm. He pours sympathy into the gap between him and his father but he pumps his passion onto the world as a whole. He learns at least a few words in all the major languages, but he doesn't feel it necessary to hitch up a welcome wagon to meet a man from Zanzibar; rather, he'll meet a man and like him and drink coffee with him and in the stride of the encounter learn that Zanzibar is where he comes from. And he won't excitedly ask him to say something! He'd carry no flag to the moon. He'd walk into any church to pray, and he'd pray without thinking to whom. These are truths for the new hero, and by being so, they direct his stride not his strife. He isn't fighting for them; he's got them. Finally, because being a world personality is about as big as he can be, he has no one else to live up to and he doesn't need an identification card.

He deals with life in person, with persons in person; you know he's all there when you're with him. He's learned that he doesn't need anyone's seal of approval to continue in his first attempt at living life. He knows nobody knows and he isn't afraid of not knowing. He cherishes his innocence. He enjoys mystery and quarrels with most solutions like a puppy tugging at a sock until it is in threads. He has much hope in the future—and is sure we'd all like one another if we'd just bury our bombs.

He believes himself to be capable to endure at any level, therefore doesn't worry about losing a job, and therefore doesn't have to adopt a role to please a boss. He has dodged those great compromises by learning to love both alternatives: job, no job, it doesn't matter, for there will soon be another job, and in the meantime, he's a good gardener. He can get along anywhere; he didn't specialize in anything except life and so he can still learn very quickly.

He's got just what everyone needs today and he can't help but give it to them: warmth and time. He's never too busy, but he always has something to do.

Those who have moved out of town, to a small village, have forgotten their TV, radio and newspaper subscriptions, but have brought their kazoos, marbles, tops, kites, jacks, and Monopoly and are attempting to get clean and simple. They are repairing their damaged personalities without America's help. I think these people know that they are living and going someplace and are excited. Disowned, suspended, kicked out, evicted—they've finally got the message that society don't want 'em subvertin' their program. They've gone, now, to live a life out of line. I've got a feeling they, too, are potential new heroes.

You see, it all comes back to what is possible for us to do in life, to accomplish, to create, to enjoy. When we systematize life we are saying that any other way outside of the system is impossible, for this and this and this will happen to you. We defend our systems by a stockade of consequences. And then somehow we forget that we created both the system and the consequences; we begin to believe the system is unchangeable, is absolute, is god. In any case, life becomes increasingly impossible outside of certain definitions, and increasingly miserable inside them. How about the exceptions, the human exceptions to the rules? For example, and this is not an extreme example even though it shocks some of us: a father wakes up in the night, his daughter is crying, he finds her suffering from some sickness, so he rushes her to the nearest, not the cheapest, hospital. At the desk they inquire: "Do you have insurance? Do you have any money? Well, I'm terribly sorry but you'll have to see our social welfare personnel and they won't be in until tomorrow morning. There's nothing I can do," she says. The twenty-five-cent paper cup. What would you do in his shoes? Or should I ask, what have you done, for I imagine all of us have run into these counter people. But most of us comply even though some rough beast is raging beneath our breath to break desks, rules and systems and more or less kidnap the help we need. But we comply, we wait for people to do it the system's way, and the clock ticks and we wait and the little girl dies in the man's arms.

And it happens all over on all levels from the grossest to the pettiest—exceptions to the rules are forced to comply. Now I put it to you, *what human being is not an exception to the rule?*

No system should ever become so rigid as to not be able to handle with ease the unexpected. Which is just another way of saying no system should not be able to handle life.

In conclusion, the new hero is out to prove to himself and others that there are ways to live where no *They* is ever blamed, where no rule is ever made that can't be unmade or changed, and where the exceptions make up the reality and beauty of being human.

Affirmation Without Absolutes

MICHAEL CASTELL*

"MY confidence is absolute. My faith is complete."

I ran across these two short sentences in a book about the history of France in the late nineteenth century.

There is a ring to the few words of these sentences which I long for. "My confidence is absolute. My faith is complete." They carry a force, a power, a feeling which I lack. Perhaps confidence and faith in our lives is what we all want. Perhaps the person who wrote those words, in 1895, in France, was stating a brave thought, a hope, and not a permanent reality, felt unwaveringly. The first human to be alone in a forest during a thunder and lightning storm, thousands of years ago, must have felt the need of the certainty those words express so deftly. From there followed a whole series of beliefs and faiths, of systems and explanations, all designed to fill the needs expressed in those words. God, geometry, beauty, order, love—all words of human desires.

Only a short time ago, I experienced what my cave-man ancestor must have felt, alone in the forest and naked to the shattering sounds.

Instead of a forest, I was in a comfortable house in a suburb of Los Angeles. The dissimilarity ends there. It was a thunder and lightning storm. I was naked and trembling, and I felt very alone. What frightened me was not the reality, as with my ancestor, but the

* *Michael Castell, age twenty-five, is a senior in the Department of Social Science, Interdisciplinary Studies. He plans to do graduate work in intellectual history and contemporary social thought. He eventually wants to teach, write and be active in some kind of community service.*

knowledge I have of a potential reality, and the consequent frustration and feeling of futility.

On a night in August, in a house near the ocean where my wife and I were visiting friends—a young married couple like ourselves—I went to bed late, after listening to music by myself. My wife and the other couple were already asleep. As I lay in bed, not quite asleep nor awake, a tremendous snap, a shattering wham! shook the house and lighted up the dark room. My first thought as I was jolted awake was that it was awfully close lightning. But it had been a clear and warm summer day, without any indication of a coming storm. Besides, there was no rain. I knew it wasn't lightning. I then heard a horn call out, like an air raid siren. We were a couple of blocks from a huge oil refinery, and I thought: maybe there's been an explosion at the refinery. Quickly then, several more shattering explosions accompanied by fizzling sounds, and an immediate flash of light filling the whole darkened house. I wasn't sure of anything by now. I got up, and as my wife was awakening I told her to get up and put something on; I thought we might have to leave the house. I went to our friends' room to wake them. By now, the explosions were louder, the house was shaking more, and the flashes of light were blinding. My friends up, we huddled in the living room, trying to decide what was happening. We decided not to use the electricity, so the house was dark. The explosions became still louder, the flashes brighter, with an accompanying sinister-sounding sizzle.

It was then that my friend said, "Maybe it's a nuclear war." I do not smile at his exaggeration, as it turned out to be, nor did I smile then. I merely said, "No. It isn't." What else could I say? And he answered, "Why not?" I didn't answer. We were all panicky and confused. Uncertainty and fear overwhelmed us. Somebody said, "Keep calm." I suggested we go to the center of the house, a small hallway, and shut the doors. I got a blanket to put over us, my friend found his transistor radio, and we huddled in the hall, doors closed, half naked, trembling. The house was rocking with the deafening, and what seemed like very near, explosions. I expected the roof to cave in any minute. I sat on the floor but got right up—I felt better standing. My wife held me and said she was scared. She was shaking. I told her, in an empty voice, to be calm. We heard little sounds all over the roof. We opened a hall door and looked through a bedroom window; it looked like rain, or maybe oil. Was it fallout?

By then my friend found a station which was on the air, and from the little box in his hands came the sound of rock and roll music. The announcer came on to say that an electric storm was going on. (Two houses and three transformers were directly hit by lightning a few blocks from where we were, which is why the flash and explosions seemed to come simultaneously. I never thought it to be lightning, after the first thunder which awakened me.)

During the period when we didn't know what to expect, I was aware of a vague but strong feeling of anger, an anger which stemmed from a total feeling of helplessness. I could not defend my wife from what was "happening" nor could I deal with it. Anger and fear were where confidence and faith should have been.

So I felt something of what early man must have experienced. But where he found God, discovered the knowable universe, I had yet to experience the worst. After I found out the source of the "danger," it was, of course, no longer frightening. The expected danger and terror had passed; there was nothing to fear. It was then, however, that I became really afraid. Not the gripping emotional fear which overwhelmed us at first, but a nagging doubt, an amorphous feeling of aloneness. I immediately realized that my terror was caused not by what was actually happening but rather by a growing and intense awareness of the world in which I live, with all its contradictions and ambivalences. I stayed up most of the rest of the night, thinking, but with no thoughts, feeling but with great vagueness; the receding storm, with its fading flashes of light and thunder, was somehow comforting.

Was my experience just another happening in the endless stream of human experiences which beset us all? Was my reaction merely mundane, common to most humans in a similar situation? But why did I have the lingering uneasiness, the quiet and vague dread that was unsettling in some unknown manner?

Perhaps what engendered this feeling in me are somewhat unique circumstances. I believe that we are undergoing a more rapid and fundamental transition in our total experiences than human beings have ever had to cope with. We are today living at the peak of this transition, at its point of no return. This confronts us with an inescapable question: What sense do we make of what is happening in our lives, and how do we orient ourselves in the light of it? This question must be answered because the traditional dualistic absolutes in terms of which Western man has heretofore interpreted the world are no longer appropriate. The old black-and-white oversimplifications are today neither sufficient as explanations of our experiences nor workable as guides to our actions. Not surprisingly, therefore, since we have lost the certainties of the past and face the openness of our future, we are haunted by conflict, ambivalence and anxiety. It is this, I think, that was triggered in me by the electrical storm in Los Angeles. And it is the same feeling—and the desire to escape or remedy it—that I believe is the key to the temper and activities of many American young people today.

The first time I questioned something I had previously taken for granted and found the answer lacking, everything else was thrown into doubt. The first time I successfully questioned what I thought to be an absolute, everything became possible. Yes and no, right and wrong, became relative, which means ambiguous. A hierarchy of values and expectations toppled. Instead of an ordered straight path up a mountain, I was faced with a rolling, curving, limitless ocean, with no left, no right, no forward and no backward. Back to the ocean I had come from, back to the mystery, the unknown, the dread, the submerged sense of oneness and aloneness. I had been raised to walk on land that no longer supported me.

I can explain this happening to myself—intellectually at least—as a result of a breakdown of dualistic, categorical thinking. For example, take the concept of East and West, or, on another level, Communism and anti-Communism. I am not here speaking of the alleged dichotomy of a "free world" ideology versus an "unfree world" ideology. As even a little reflection will show, those labels are too superficial, too far removed from reality, to have any meaning at all. What I am talking about is the current postures of both the "Western" and "Eastern" worlds being pitted against each other in an allegedly uncompromisable death struggle for survival. At least two things are absurd about this posture. In the first place, as is becoming increasingly evident, the peoples of both these power blocks—regardless of their ideologies—are pursuing the same basic human objectives and encountering the same kinds of problems. And secondly, as is true of all nations and peoples today, they have in various ways become so interdependent that they have no viable alternative but to accept the legitimacy of one another's existence. Whereas it may still be possible for an individual to live as an island, such a self-centered and blind logic is out of the question for major world powers. If the United States is to survive, Red China also has to be allowed to live as it sees fit; and vice versa. One nation cannot impose conditions on another that it itself would not accept. The world has grown too small for this, and weapons too powerful. The bomb has brought us together under a common destiny; it is all together or none at all.

Understandably, nations are finding it difficult to accommodate themselves to these new realities. Peoples have lived by a brute survival ethic for thousands of years. It has been man against nature, man against man. Ideologies were built and attitudes were deified to justify whatever seemed to further tribal survival. The world consisted of friends and enemies. And perhaps there were times when this was possible and even necessary. But it clearly is no longer so today. Nor is it moral. It implies nothing more than a glorified robber philosophy. "My country right or wrong" has to be enlarged to a more universal logic and loyalty: "Our world, may she always be right, because otherwise we're all hurting."

With this rather relativistic and independent world view I have inevitably come into a conflict of loyalties in my own personal life. What does a man do when his own beliefs and those of his society, as expressed by his government, do not accord? How does he act when what his government professes to be necessary and right (usually in that order) and what he himself sees as moral and in mankind's best interest do not coincide?

This dilemma is not new. In all ages there have been individuals in conflict with the predominant tenor of their times. But today there are fewer alternatives. The alternatives in the past have been escape, resistance—with or without protesting—and rebellion. But escape has for all practical purposes become impossible. The world is too small and the bomb too overwhelming. There are no more Wests to move to. There is no way a man can physically disappear. And even if to disappear were possible, it would be an act of moral irresponsibility.

Another circumstance that makes escape impossible as a solution to individual conflict with society—for me, at least—is that I am *of* America; my roots are here and it is within the American experience that I must define my identity. It has therefore not been easy to go against enforced national attitudes. I have the capacity for patriotism, and perhaps even a need to express such feelings. My first reaction upon hearing of John Kennedy's death was to cry. I was a little surprised afterward—since I had not particularly identified with this president and had protested some of his policies—but I guess he was my president after all, if more unconsciously than consciously.

What frustrates my capacity for patriotism and identification with American policies is that the mainstream of American politics is operating in terms of assumptions and objectives that are no longer able to facilitate meaningful human growth, either within all the countries of the world or among them. The United States government's effort to absolutize these historically provincial American standards and to insist upon their universal acceptance seems to me both impractical and immoral. It is an effort, moreover, that is being resisted by more and more young people even in the United States. Time was when the preoccupation of Americans was so intensely with achieving economic and social success within the traditional American definitions that it did not occur to them—and quite understandably, I might add—to question these particular interpretations as to what life was about. But the growth of abundance, increased education, and the trend of world affairs is changing all this. At least in the "have" countries today, young people are no longer unquestioningly "buying" such unhistorical and ethnocentric responses to life. The questions are no longer how to "make it," how to compete successfully in the world of commerce, or how to reach the top of the heap socially. The question now is, where do we find our meanings—and this in such a way to be compatible with the quest for meaning of all other peoples as well.

More and more, in the industrially developed nations, we are able to take the satisfaction of our physical wants for granted. The challenge now is to explore what we may need and be capable of beyond mere animal existence. How do we extend our prosperity to everyone? How do we use it in a humanly fulfilling and dignifying way? These are the real questions. And they cannot be answered in the framework of our traditional conceptions. To continue imposing these conceptions on our present experiences is to limit ourselves and, in effect, to distrust our own capabilities. Henceforth the need is not to define human relationships in terms of prior standards, no matter how sanctified, but to derive new standards that are suggested by the personal and social possibilities of the human relationships themselves.

The transition to a world where ideas are in the service of life, rather than where life is subordinated to absolutized ideas, is bound to be slow and painful. It demands an unprecedented combination of courage, imagination and responsibility. For it requires a most sober reappraisal of many of our most cherished ideas as well as institutions.

It is in the perspective of this transition that one must understand the growing dissatisfaction with the old capitalistic ethic. This view of human purposes and functioning is too narrow; it doesn't do justice to what people feel their lives are about. We are no longer satisfied to be conceived of as mere producers and consumers, joyfully competing against one another in an orgy of righteous ambition, infused with a fascination for things and occasionally taking time out for spiritual and cultural injections to avoid the stigma of crass materialism. The big companies themselves are doing the job of rejecting capitalism. IBM Corporation, considered to be a leader in personnel operations, will help an employee have children, educate them, buy a bomb shelter, and have himself buried. Big business and big labor are still behind the times in that they continue to concentrate on comfort and security, but gradually increasing importance is being attached to how what one does affects one's sensibilities and enriches one's life, rather than on what is actually being produced. Life is no longer a straight and narrow path to a definable goal, but a symphony of experience, with each movement, each note, something worth-while to savor, and the end not the goal, but the consummation of an enjoyable experience, a letdown at that. I suspect that life never really was best conceptualized as a path to climb up—to reach the top of a mountain; people have been taking side trips all along, and now the side trips are becoming institutionalized and respected.

By necessity this is a slow process and involves initial excesses of negativity. An institutionalized standard doesn't give easily, even when its efficacy is dated. It is first pushed and pulled until it is stretched out of shape, and a new entity suddenly emerges, often without the conscious consent of those doing the pushing and pulling. The general direction is freedom and sensitivity in human values. The struggle often becomes irreversible and rigid because of the negativity that inevitably accompanies the first steps to reject what was once useful and meaningful.

To be caught in a culture which is unacceptable but yet inescapable leads to resistance. The question to be answered for us in this position is how to resist. It is not one thing, one body politic, which it is necessary to resist. It is everything that threatens our lives, our opportunity to experience what we want—and what our neighbor might want to experience. It is all that dehumanizes the world we live in—all those forces that work against an evolving set of values big enough to accommodate us all and stable enough to insure the minimum amount of confidence needed. Words like dehumanization and alienation are kicked around everywhere, but it is no accident that they are invoked so often. They refer to something significant, subtle and not easy to explain.

How our conventional culture does less than justice to human needs, experiences and complexities can nowhere be seen more clearly than on commercial television. Especially in the commercials. I am thinking of two of these in particular, both advertising body deodorants. The word itself, deodorant, means to reduce something human—to dehumanize a certain kind of smell. One commercial advocates the use of its deodorant to "take the worry out of closeness." How fortunate it would be if that were the only problem we had in being close to one another! The other commercial suggests the perfect family deodorant: all members of the family can use it because "nothing touches but the spray." I guess the roll-on type might roll on too much of something or other. How can you fight that? Personally, I'm prepared to share my roll-on—if I had any—with anybody. I even get some satisfaction in using one toothbrush for my wife and myself. My father once gave me a new toothbrush when he learned we had only one. I accepted it and secretly threw out the old one. But if the culture is becoming mechanized and antiseptic, it's not going to matter much if I defiantly keep one toothbrush. I can't brush my teeth all day.

How to constructively change what needs changing? This is the question that impinges most immediately on the socially and politically involved student. It always comes up, in one form or another, whenever those "on to what's happening" get together. That we are getting together to discuss this question is valuable in itself. And so are our various efforts to do something about it. Admittedly, many of these efforts are clumsy and ineffective. Our critics point this out and yet they overlook what we are trying to do. Of course we must make mistakes. What we are fighting is so huge and ambiguous that it demands many different starting points, tactics and solutions. As always in such creative, transitional situations, there is no way to learn and accomplish anything except by honest trial and error.

It is hard to grasp the possibilities, directions, problems and implications of this vast cultural revolution. Most of my energies are involved in this process, and once I had committed myself to it as a conscious participant, I became vulnerable to many anxieties and a frequent feeling of futility. It has been hard to fight against the feeling that I was leading a peripheral existence.

An experience I had might make what I am trying to say clearer. My wife and I spent most of one summer traveling through Mexico. While in a small town near central Mexico, we stayed at a hotel where there were several other Americans, all of them students. A couple were from New York and the rest from the Bay area. We were an assorted lot yet had much in common because we all had reacted to the same subtle forces at work in America; we all had rebelled from, and rejected part of, American culture. Even though we had not met before, there was an immediate group identity; undoubtedly this was helped by the fact that we were Americans in a foreign country, but it went beyond that. We recognized in one another common symptoms and common allegiances. In varying degrees we each were radical, cynical, sensitive, tolerant of ambiguity, creative, irreligious but somewhat reverent, and all of us, in some manner, running scared. The experience I want to relate is a conversation which we had as a group one evening. What was actually said by each person has grown dim in my memory, but the general mood and my reactions are well remembered, as the conversation encompassed, at one time or another, what is happening today and the forms which resistance is taking. There was no group consensus, just as there is no group consensus among student movements today; it's just not that simple. (An easy answer to today's student unrest doesn't exist—whether there are 17.8 percent Communists in some so-called revolutionary student groups or not. Communism and Americanism are not the question; both are meaningless labels on their face, and as such I dislike both. The only "ism" which counts is humanism.)

The general topic that evening was what does one do when caught up in a culture from which one feels alienated, in a culture one feels is going in the wrong direction. A rather vague feeling, but real. On a much smaller scale, I experienced this feeling when I caught an express bus in the outer limits of San Francisco, going downtown. I was standing on a street where the express bus doesn't normally stop, but the bus driver stopped anyway, and since it was late and raining I felt really in luck. After the bus rode the freeway and exited in downtown San Francisco, I rang the buzzer to get off after his first stop in the downtown area. To my surprise, I was informed that the bus makes only one stop downtown and then continues on an express route to another section of town. I asked the driver if he could let me off. No, he couldn't, and as I stood by the stairs waiting for the bus to go another two miles beyond where I was going, I felt alienated from the whole damn bus.

When the entire culture is going in a direction I don't want, it's hard to decide on alternatives. Some people get off, get a different bus, for a different trip. One of my friends in the hotel room was getting off and taking a different trip. It is an inward trip, via Zen, drugs, and a rejection of an outer reality which was untenable for some good reasons, as he expressed them. He proceeded to explain verbally how senseless and useless verbal communication is; we can't communicate without being caught in the games of language. Withdraw from the game, discover yourself, expand your consciousness, and existence ceases to be problematic. Don't ask how because it can't be explained; you have to be "there"—and when "there" you know it; it doesn't have to be explained and can't be explained. It is beyond reason. Along this vein, we often hear the expression, "trust your guts." I one time had a difficult decision to make concerning the military draft, and while discussing this with a friend, he said, "Well, whatever decision you make, make it from here," and pointed to my stomach. This speaks of a distrust of reason, a lack of faith in the mind. In the sense that there is more that influences man than conscious rationality, this lack of faith is legitimate. The Enlightenment, where reason was to be applied to social problems, has not brought enlightenment. When one hears someone say, "Now let's be reasonable," it is often a preface to selling out. In part though, it is a reaction to the dualism of mind and body; there really is no separateness to these two entities, although Western man has been trying to separate them for a long time and still is trying to do so. The perfect separation would be a mindless human body tending a perfect think machine, the forerunners of which are in existence now. To free reason from the body completely would be the ultimate dehumanization. To negate the value of the mind, on the other hand, is also a lessening of human potentiality. To turn inward and to retreat from verbal communication is ultimately antisocial and is becoming impossible to maintain. The dualism between the private realm and the public realm is collapsing. It can be maintained only at great psychic cost. What affects the Vietnamese affects us—perhaps someday directly, but even now we can't help but respond to the horror on television reels. If we harden ourselves, which most do, we are frustrating our capacity for compassion; on the other hand, if we reacted spontaneously to the horror each time we confronted it, we would perhaps drain our capacity for compassion. Either alternative is lacking. In a crowded world, there is no personal salvation without social salvation, and vice versa. We must plan for social justice, as a whole, and at the same time allow for individual freedom. Obviously, there is a dilemma involved here. It is a dilemma, but not a dichotomy; it is not socialism versus free enterprise, nor Communism versus freedom. It is not a question of ends, but a question of means. Which means will allow a maximum of freedom with the necessary minimum of stability? This is the question facing both the public and private realms.

Another alternative is rebellion, but is this a real alternative? The rebel in the group claimed that things were going to be different come this fall. He said he was a different type of rebel. Economic, social, and political rebellion wasn't enough. What is really needed is a spiritual rebellion. And how is this spiritual revolution to come about? Billy Graham has been trying for some time, with a lot of people, without too much success as far as I can see. "But," my friend answered, "this revolution will be brought about through acid." So I get this picture of a struggling Nixon being held down while someone injects him with a consciousness-expanding drug. I think I might run the other way before it took effect. No, I said to my friend, I don't think it's a practical idea—it's sort of fascinating to think of going around with a drug-gun, pointing it at public figures and saying, as you pull the trigger, "Zap! You're high!" and then watching them turn into harmonious human beings, at peace with the universe and their souls. But it would just be another drug-induced "brave new world." It's going to be hard enough to get enough people to take a birth control pill, let alone a consciousness-expanding trip. He has a good point though—violent revolution, even if possible and warranted, which I don't believe it is, without a spiritual revolution, would be of no ultimate good; but a spiritual revolution cannot be brought about violently.

So I'm left with a moving undecidedness; each new encounter elicits a response—most of the responses are negative. Sartre was perhaps right when he wrote that an individual's freedom is ultimately negative. The one freedom which cannot be taken away is the freedom to say no. It is a freedom which is aptly named. But it is negative, and the human spirit deserves more.

I want more. Either we build more, or we will be destroyed. If not physically destroyed by a technology run amuck, or a military force run amuck, then spiritually destroyed by a deadening of that joy of life which is so fleeting, so resistant to being held in one place, and, though eternal, so fragile.

I am left with myself and my resources. I demonstrate; I say no more war and have the feeling I am affecting no more than the Hell's Angels, and even them not positively or creatively. But yet I am held by the feeling that if enough people say no more war, before they say anything else, then there will be no more war. I tutor so-called culturally deprived children and am overwhelmed by the problems I encounter; when I multiply the problems to the majority of those alive today, I am more overwhelmed. Yet I am held by the glimmering of a joyful force, a greatness which breaks through, ever so often, the layers of restraint, the twists and turns of a confusing and harsh existence.

I am sustained by a faith in my own humanness, and I affirm this by recognizing the humanness in others.

What sustains me forces me into a personal dichotomy. My faith in my humanness, which I never fail to see in others, no matter how buried, leads me to react to my world. I say no killing in Vietnam, but I realize the world doesn't operate on this level. I am forced to interpret and criticize on political and social levels. I can do this well enough, but I cannot find faith in these arguments. The counter-arguments are just as convincing to those who hold them. It is as though I live on two levels: one moral, warm, and human, the other artificial and abstract. I walk with a foot in each world, straddling the periphery of both. But I walk with an eye to each.

It has taken me years to be able to say no; I do not plan on taking years to say yes. I join with others who are saying yes, and with them look for and help create, with all the warmth and understanding which moves within me, what has become a necessity to create.

What we look for, and what we want to help create, is a social order, a human order, which allows for and encourages meaningfulness in our experiences, demanding independence for the individual and tolerance in the whole; a great society, moving not toward a narrow orthodoxy, but expanding outward, with room for all our personal hierarchies of values, of whatever dimensions. Its conditions are trust and relatedness of respect and freedom—a worthy search, which should be welcomed by all of concerned heart and sensitive mind. It speaks of an affirmation of life without the deadening effects of absolutes.

From Youth Culture to Commitment

ALLEN CHERRY*

MUCH turmoil during the past two years has been experienced on our college and university campuses. There has been a great deal of bafflement as to the sources of this student unrest, and many people have reacted to it with indignation and hostility. Yet this discontent and its expression appear to me entirely natural. For the fact is that the realities of our lives and the ideas and institutions by which we are trying to live have grown more and more out of line. And it is understandable that where these disparities are, so to speak, put under the microscope—that is, on our college and university campuses—they should also occasion the greatest pain and concern. Intellectual probing and social activism among today's students are therefore not the product of immature collegians, trouble-making malcontents, or youthful subversives. They are an expression of the most serious, responsible, and practical-minded soul-searching.

Our colleges and universities have for long been identified with the ideal of academic freedom. Yet while these institutions have eloquently advocated this ideal, they have, in fact, failed fully to exercise it. They have been satisfied to uphold the status quo and, at most, to provide scholarly commentary on our lives. It is for this reason that they have of late found it increasingly difficult to handle the motivations and activities of their students. For while these young people are grateful for our heritage and generally respect scholarly efforts, they

* *Allen Cherry received his B.A. in January, 1966, from the Department of Social Science, Interdisciplinary Studies, at San Francisco State College. He is currently with the Peace Corps in Nigeria. He plans to go on to graduate school to get a Ph.D. in Social Welfare.*

believe that our society today needs much more. They are committed to cultural progress and insist on using academic freedom to do whatever they can to facilitate it. The immediate result has been conflicts on our college and university campuses. Yet these conflicts are merely symptoms. The underlying ailment is society-wide in scope. The problem is how more effectively to use our resources to build the kind of country that more and more of us today believe is desirable and possible. And in confronting this problem, academic communities have an essential role. They must give up the safety of mere classroom commentary and scholarly publication and be prepared to involve themselves in the mainstream of contemporary life.

The reasons students are today pressing their colleges and universities to enter the struggle for cultural reforms go back to our grade-school years. It is then that we first learn the ideals that we later come to believe can and must be implemented: that our way of life is the best possible; that democracy in the American sense represents the culmination of man's search for a perfect social and political system; that our elected government is fair and judicious in its dealings with Americans; and that as a nation we follow policies best designed to further peace and human fulfillment throughout the world. The children who have taken these grade-school lessons most seriously, later on become the most idealistic and socially concerned college and university students. And it is then these same young people—ironically, the most successful products of our earlier educational conditioning—to whom the discrepancies between our ideals and realities come as the greatest disappointments.

How is a student to deal with his growing realization of the many profound inconsistencies between what we say we are and what we actually are? Normally, he does one of two things. Either he retains his confidence in the status quo, accepting popular rationalizations for the differences between our ideals and realities. Or he accepts the responsibility of trying to help bridge the gap between what he believes America ought to be and what he sees it actually is. If he chooses the latter course, he soon comes to be known as an activist, agitator, protester, or even Communist—depending mostly on the preconceptions of whoever is doing the labeling.

Those who adopt the commitment to do something to further

constructive social change immediately face the problem of exactly how to go about it. College students have little political or economic leverage. The only realistic strategy open to them is therefore to band together with other students who have the conviction to be unpopular and attempt to build a constituency of their own. In order to do this, they must somehow enlist the support of whoever among the general public may share their concerns. And the most obvious and economical way of doing this, is, of course, the protest demonstration.

There are, however, certain shortcomings of the demonstration which have bothered me. First of all, the demonstration may already have been overused. When you have a number of demonstrations, all going on at the same time and all aimed at different objectives, they are inevitably going to detract from one another's impact.

A second misgiving I have about the protest demonstrations is that owing to popular misunderstandings they often backfire. Instead of evoking sympathy, they incur the public's wrath. Often it is not the issue itself that antagonizes the public, nor even the tactics of the demonstrators. It is the fact that college students tend to overintellectualize the points they are trying to make. Many people who at heart may agree with the demonstrators but who have not gone to college may as a result not understand what is being protested against. They may even be offended by these "smart aleck" college kids and suspect they are trying to pull a fast one on them. In consequence, people who ought to be working together with the protesters end up opposed to them.

Another drawback of the protest demonstration is that it inevitably appears extremist in nature. It is obviously not extreme to those actually involved in it. But then, the members of the John Birch Society don't consider themselves extremists either. What I mean is that since demonstrations are directed against some aspect of the status quo, they have a tendency to provoke an equally vociferous reaction on the part of those who feel threatened. Discussion of the issues thus becomes polarized. It is carried on by two committed and informed groups, over the heads of the general public which for the most part refuses to be committed to anything save its self-interest and which is often too uninformed correctly to determine even that.

Why then, with all these disadvantages, do demonstrations continue on and off campuses all over the country? The answer, as I have already suggested, lies in the inability of student activists to affect contemporary life through any of the established channels. Though most students are undoubtedly better informed about our society's institutions and issues than are their parents, they for the most part are not yet of voting age. And even to those who are, one, a hundred or even a thousand votes seem to constitute very little real influence in a nation of nearly two hundred million people. Though demonstrations are open to many objections, they therefore nevertheless offer some attractiveness. Aside from whatever effectiveness they may or may not have, they at least enable those who participate in them to take a stand on their principles and to bring their views to the public's attention. And this, after all, is in the finest American tradition.

When I was a child and asked questions, my parents did not always give me simple answers. And often their advice was difficult to live up to. Though I didn't fully understand it at the time, I know now that what they were trying to teach me is what we broadly call integrity. They were encouraging in me the ability to make my own decisions, based on my own feelings and beliefs and not necessarily those of my friends, peers or neighbors. On most occasions while I was growing up, this ideal of living by my own convictions posed no serious dilemmas. For in effect, I continued to live largely by my father's prescriptions. Though he always urged me to be confident in myself, he had so much strength and confidence of his own that I rarely had the opportunity to confront life as an independent individual. It wasn't until I was in high school that I began to move in my own directions, even though these weren't very healthy directions in any respect other than they they were now my own and no longer those of my father. It was also at that time, I believe, that I began to suspect that his earlier emphasis on total honesty and integrity represented a more important key to success as a human being than his subsequent concern with self-confidence, whether his own or mine. I should add one other note in this connection. During all my conflicts with my father—which, I believe, were no more serious than those of any other rather independent male youngster and a strong-willed, middle-class-oriented father—I received considerable support from my mother. It was not that she agreed with my point of view, for she almost never did. I suspect that whenever she to some extent went along with my minor rebellions it was because my father's uncompromising attitude somewhat "bugged" her too.

My biggest problem at this point was that my rebellions were in the form of a good time. Throughout my last two years of high school and my first two years at college, I was a confirmed playboy, with nothing more serious on my mind than where the next party was to be and how I was going to get the booze for it (since I was still underage); however, I usually managed to overcome obstacles such as these.

In January of 1961, after three lighthearted semesters at San Francisco State College, the administration no longer felt disposed to put up with my less-than-minimum efforts, and I was disqualified—the current euphemism for "flunked out." I promptly enrolled in a junior college, which provided for me an experience of immeasurable worth. I had been surrounded at San Francisco State by a student body composed of generally serious, intense people. True, it had not affected me while I was there, but upon attending this junior college the contrast was like a slap in the face. The vast majority of the students at the college acted exactly as I remembered my high-school contemporaries had, and I was shocked into a realization of my own immaturity and extremely anxious to get out of that atmosphere and return to what seemed to me a great deal more vital environment. I stayed there only one semester and then, because it was impossible to make up all my grade points in that time, I went to work and attended night school for two semesters. I then returned to San Francisco State.

My decision to get out of my parents' house and work for a year was probably the most valuable one I ever made. I learned more about people and their contradictions during this period than I could have hoped to from all the psychology and sociology courses offered anywhere. I worked for a fairly small, self-contained merchandising firm dealing in audio-visual equipment, but the most valuable lessons I learned there had nothing to do with the products handled. I was struck by the ineffectualness of so many of the individuals I found in the business community. These people professed self-confidence but just couldn't do much of anything right. They always seemed to have some rationalization at hand for their failure, or else they would manage to place the blame on someone lower on the ladder. Another characteristic of these frustrated individuals struck me: they were the ones who always screamed the loudest about how they had made their own way in the world and how everyone else should have to fight the same battle. They were all bigots in one way or another, whether it was race, social status, or some other characteristic which they chose as a target for their frustrations. I also met some people in the business community who were competent, sensitive and intelligent. And I was encouraged to note that these individuals, whether politically liberal or conservative, were quite often concerned about other people, a trait not common among the other group. These more competent people, I also observed, were not afraid to accept the responsibility of an unpopular decision or stand, whereas the former types would never put themselves in such jeopardy. In my continuing contact with American society I have found these conclusions to hold true rather generally.

It was, then, at this point that I returned to San Francisco State College. I felt a different need than I had before, and I began to search out a different type of individual for my friends. I also chose my classes with a different criterion, though I still had no definite goal in mind. And I began to read with a different and more inquiring look at the material. I found a great deal of help from Nikos Kazantzakis, whose books seemed to articulate what I had myself begun to feel about man's life and its relation to the world. I found in Kazantzakis an appreciation of everything truly human, even our less-than-perfect emotional make-up. I found a love of life so expansive that it made me realize just how limited one man's life must be, and how important it is for us to experience as much as we possibly can without worrying too much about the outcome. All of a sudden a lot of pieces seemed to fit together, though it was some time before they really began to make sense to me. I got married and dropped out of school for another year so that my wife could finish up first, since she was closer to her degree than I. This time I worked in a tire shop. This afforded me constant, intimate contact with the general public, and I found that what I had observed earlier on a small scale was now repeated for me on a wide screen. I noticed especially how petty and "hung up" on inconsequential material things our culture has become.

Upon my return to San Francicso State College I was confronted with the decision as to what I was going to do. I had come to believe that I had to do something, not merely work for someone. I thought of perhaps going into psychology, since I was interested in rehabilitative work of some sort. I also considered teaching, but was afraid that I wouldn't be able to stomach the restrictions of a public school classroom. Then I came into contact with a faculty group on this campus who, I felt, saw the world in the same relativistic, eclectic and vital way that I did. They advocated an interdisciplinary view, combining a lot of different perspectives and denying the existence of any absolute system with which to explain reality. At about the same time I became involved in youth work with delinquent boys in the East Bay.[1]

Since taking on this rehabilitative work it has become increasingly clear to me that the relativistic and open-ended way of looking at life that I have somehow arrived at is the only one dynamic enough, and allowing enough room for human complexities, to enable me to be of any use to these youngsters. It is never any single factor of our culture which has led them into conflict. It is always some unique combination of circumstances that has somehow interacted with their own particular psychological make-up. What they all want more than anything else is a comfortable and trusting relationship with an adult. And so it is essential that the adults in question be fairly broad-based people who have a sufficient sense of what is going on at different levels of our society to be able to introduce the youngsters into workable human relationships with as little pain as possible. But unfortunately ours is a society of pigeonholers. We like everything specialized. Yet the fact is that only a few of all the boys and girls who are defined as delinquents require specialized treatment. The rest need only humanization—the ability to live with other people without fear.

In our affluent Western societies, and particularly in the United States, we have in the past couple of decades developed a unique kind of youth culture in which young people must hang in unproductive

[1] The area eastward and across the Bay from San Francisco, comprising chiefly the adjoining cities of Berkeley and Oakland.

limbo from the time they are about thirteen until they reach the magic age of twenty-one. We expect them to control their own behavior, yet we deny them the responsibility of working out for themselves what this behavior should be. It is a case of the same old paradox of the eighteen-year-old boy who is held old enough to fight and perhaps die for his country, but who isn't considered grown-up enough to be allowed a voice in deciding exactly what it is he may be called upon to die for. Since the youth has no personally meaningful responsibilities—as he once had in being needed to contribute to the survival of his family—he cleaves to his friends who are in the same boat. Together they then develop their own values, codes of ethics and dress, all of which are often in conflict with those of the official world of the adults. Such reactions against the expectations of the adult community seem to me entirely understandable. But they do create serious problems of communication. These problems are further aggravated by the resentments adults tend to feel at being excluded from the youth culture. The result is often a communications no man's land which neither group can penetrate.

Some of the boys with whom I have contact are so far removed from what we consider normal values and ideals that it is hard to believe we all grew up in the same country. The fact is, of course, that we haven't grown up in the same society at all; these youngsters come from several subcultures other than the middle-class one from which most of our values and ideals stem. To make things worse, there are then a number of youth sub-subcultures, and these obviously remove the youngsters even further from our society's main stream. It is this gap that concerned adults must somehow bridge. The youngsters can't do it themselves for the simple reason that they haven't been there. This is where I feel my commitment must be.

I have said that I want to contribute to tangible, constructive changes in our society and that I doubt the effectiveness of the demonstration as a tool for this purpose. The more I become involved with the youngsters I have mentioned, the more convinced I am of the urgency of getting through to them as full human beings. It's true that no great societal transformations are going to take place because of my contacts with a few disturbed kids. But I can hope that by succeeding in my limited efforts I can help these young people communicate better with their peers, with the world around them, and later on with their own children.

If our interested, responsible teachers were allowed to use contemporary materials realistically geared to children's backgrounds and potentialities, the public schools could give youngsters the start they need to develop constructive tie-ins with the bigger society of which they need to be a part. But the schools appear to me to reflect too much of the community's attitude of disrespect for youngsters as individuals. And to make matters worse, most teachers, I suspect, are actually afraid of their students.

I have given a great deal of thought as to what directions my life is to take. I have had to clarify my self-image, in regard both to the world as it is and as I hope it will be.

First of all and most importantly, I must be committed, in a serious, adult sense, to something in which I genuinely believe and which in some manner will improve the human condition. Past generations have had wars to which they could devote themselves to help "free the world." Today though we may be fighting somewhere in Southeast Asia, it is to no good end, for the only possible "end" of any fighting we do now is self-destruction, and this is unthinkable. If we are going to do anything for the world it must therefore be for people as people. And as I have indicated, my own most likely part in this effort will be rehabilitative work with youngsters.

Secondly, I have found that it is terribly important to me that I be effective in whatever capacity I find myself. One reason I am concerned about this is that I have come in contact with so many ineffective people, people who probably because they themselves unconsciously recognized their impotence, were also generally obstructionists. Another reason I am hypersensitive on this point is that a great many of the really ineffective individuals I have met have been members of bureaucracies. If I follow my present interests, I am inevitably going to be working in, or along with, one type of bureaucracy or another. I feel that my best defense against the inefficiency that seems to be endemic to it is to be ever aware of its dangers.

Lastly but no less importantly, I hope that I never become so encapsulated in my routines, habits and attitudes that I forget how to live. I have watched many people—including my parents and even some of my friends at their comparatively young ages—become more and more involved in an ever smaller portion of life. As they grow older, their world seems constantly to shrink. This is the exact opposite of what I consider the natural course of life to be. As your scope of knowledge increases, so should your capacity for accommodating to new experiences. I can only attribute people's failure to exercise this capacity to some kind of fear. And I believe that this fear is at the very heart of the many inhibiting "hang-ups" which the adult community in this country displays in its frequently irrational handling of individual, national as well as international problems.

Why is it that a fairly normal, not very brave individual such as myself can speak with any confidence at all about accomplishing these goals, in a society apparently as mixed-up as ours? It is because I feel that the times are changing. There are now visible encouraging new trends. They are progresssive, dynamic and humanizing trends that promise fundamental alterations in our entire orientation. They are not going to happen fast enough for some of us, but the changes are taking place. One can cite many substantial examples. In most of our states, for example, the rightness of capital punishment is being seriously questioned. Not only angry outsiders but an ever greater number of responsible citizen groups have come to protest the war in Vietnam. Legal procedures are being amended in order to better recognize and facilitate the rights of individuals of all classes and ethnic groups. Government is slowly beginning to face up to the importance of reinvesting our affluence in human beings through new kinds of social programs. And there are increasing pressures for the United States to give aid to emerging nations without inhibiting or undignifying strings that these other peoples cannot afford to accept. All these examples point in a hopeful direction. They are evidences of a more creative and humanly respectful American philosophy. Conservative elements in our country try to deny the presence of these trends, but if they only look around they must be able to see that they exist and that they are, in fact, irreversible. I myself am deeply encouraged by these new directions, extremely depressed when they are retarded, and hopeful that they will continue.

If, then, we are making progress, the question has to be asked:

progress toward what? For we must have some kind of image in our minds of the kind of life we hope will become possible. Perhaps the most immediate way to answer this question is to suggest some of the conditions one would like to see assured for one's children.

Besides what my wife and I may be able to do for them as parents, I believe that my children's most significant experience ought to be their formal schooling. I hope it will be the kind of education that stimulates and nourishes all their innate curiosity both about themselves and the world around them. If this is to be accomplished, our grade schools must be more realistically attuned to our contemporary values and circumstances than they generally are today. They must do a better job than they have in the past of enabling children to discover and accept themselves, of helping them to fit understandingly into their peer groups, but also of retaining as much as possible of their own unique, self-directing individualities.

And if these things are not done for them in the earlier years of their education, I hope that my children will, as did I, find the necessary insights and encouragement at college. I hope that they will encounter someone with whom they can communicate not only about academics but life in general, and so develop soundly-based confidence in themselves and in the possibilities of the world as a whole. For it is of utmost importance that the relation between student and faculty member be a dynamic, open and intimate one. It is only in this way that the inexperienced student can be properly stimulated to use his own mind. Since parents apparently cannot or will not do it, it is up to the teacher to invest youngsters with the self-confidence they need to use their minds in an original manner. This is not something we just do in our culture; left to ourselves, we tend to follow along the simplest and most trodden path possible. Yet unless there is at least a large minority sufficiently emancipated and stimulated to employ their faculties with some creativity, there can be no progress and life will be terribly drab.

Teachers with the motivations and personal skills required for this kind of one-to-one educational contact are, unfortunately, rather rare. It is therefore necessary to set up the academic process so as to maximize such educational benefits institutionally. At San Francisco State College, for example, we have a sequence of introductory courses called General Education. Approximately sixty units of these are required for graduation. They represent an honest attempt to acquaint the student with the subject matter and perspectives of many academic disciplines. For the most part, however, I have found these courses have, in practice, become drudgery for professors and students alike. They must now be reappraised and made lively and interesting once again through imaginative instruction, use of less standardized and more relevant materials, and smaller, more informal classes. This is of highest importance, for these courses offer the student the only exposure to the larger knowledge he needs to discover himself and to guide his subsequent intellectual inquiry.

The most vital goal that I have in mind for my own generation and the next is peace. And here, too, education has a crucial role to play. We must look to our schools to train us to see our contemporary realities in their true complexities and in historical perspective. And we must depend on them to help us think critically and constructively as well as to sensitize us to our human opportunities and responsibilities. Only to the extent such greater knowledge and humane dedication permeate our society from its grass roots to its government will we be able to solve our problems at home and do more than pay lip service to the cause of peace and welfare abroad.

In writing these pages I have had one underlying purpose, which I hope has become clear. I have wanted to explain that many college students today are no longer content merely to go to class, graduate, get a job, and watch television every night for the rest of their lives. Many of us are committed to the progress of this country and, eventually, of the international community which will inevitably arise as the world grows smaller. We may not be as articulate in a rhetorical sense as were some of our predecessors. But we are more alert. And instead of just trusting in progress, we are committed to finding concrete and appropriate actions to help bring it about. The world is going to change; society is going to improve; and we are anxious to be a part of this.

Beyond Categories

JANET SPEARS SCHAEFER*

I would say my education began when I started to change my general outlook and to think more for myself. This means that what I call my education started after approximately eleven years of public school, that schooling having had virtually nothing to do with the beginnings of my real education. Upon the completion of junior high school I was able to read and write, had come to know my times tables, spelling, rudimentary elements of composition and grammar, the simple arithmetical operations and a greatly simplified version of United States and world history. But far more important, I had also acquired a way of looking at the world—you might call it a set of attitudes, or the sum of my opinions, or just the foundations of thought which enabled me to interpret events and find meaning in my life. We use our basic education only as a means of getting along in life; we must all know how to read, add and subtract, to write letters. But we really live by our outlook. It is our attitudes toward our fellow man, toward our government, about economics, about religion that really determine how we experience things, what meaning we find in life.

Perhaps what I mean will become more clear with this example: a former boss of mine and I used to have frequent conversations about things that were currently in the news. His way of seeing the world was totally different from mine, and this difference was nowhere more

* *Janet Spears Schaefer, age twenty-two, is a junior in the Department of Social Science, Interdisciplinary Studies. She plans to continue her formal education at graduate school in the areas of cultural history, the fine arts and contemporary literature.*

evident than in our individual reactions to the same bit of news. Once an article appeared in the paper about Negro riots and his reaction was, "How do these people ever hope to get respect when they do things like that?" To him, the riots were clearly an act of irresponsibility and willfulness. I told him I thought the rioters were expressing their frustration at being second-class citizens, at always getting the leftover jobs (or no jobs at all), at rarely, if ever, being accepted as plain human beings, neither rejected nor patronized. We were both reacting to the same set of facts and the facts were charged with significance for each of us. But the significance was different for both of us since the meaning we each found was related to our basic attitudes.

To take another example: an article about a gang fight appeared in the paper. There have been numerous publications in the last couple of decades about the general rise in juvenile delinquency and my boss must have had these in mind when he saw this particular article, for he sighed, "What is this world coming to?" According to his way of thinking, crime is an indicator of degeneracy. Very simply, the more crime, the worse the moral state of society. The same story makes me think of several things, but none are related to morality or degeneracy. I think of crime as indicative of a breakdown of social institutions, of adverse economic conditions and of inappropriate culturally defined goals. If I were to voice a counterpart reaction it might be, "Where is this world going? How is it changing?"

Everyone has a way of seeing the world regardless of the amount of formal schooling he has had. One's outlook has to do with what he has learned from his family, friends and school, and what he has learned from himself—that is, his own personal experiences. Some individuals can go through college and find that their total outlook is only slightly modified from that with which they grew up. Such persons find that for the most part, the ideas they got from their parents and from precollege schools are reinforced. Others may feel that the combination of social and academic experiences they have encountered while at college have changed their lives radically. I personally fall into the latter group. About the time I entered my middle teens, my personal experiences started to cause me to have to change many of my basic attitudes. What I call my education began at that time: it started with a few initial doubts; it grew into some important personal ethical questions, such as "Am I a moral person considering my conduct?" and "Do I believe in a religion and a God?"; and it has since progressed to my deciding for myself the answers to some of these questions, using what I have experienced, read and learned in college to help me do so. Having found that the outlook I grew up with was simply untenable in most respects, I became a more searching and more critical person. As I searched (and am still searching) to find the most appropriate way of seeing things, education took on the special significance it has for me. I began to look upon my schooling not just as something I was expected to do or only as something that would help me find a better job but also, and more importantly, as a period of study that would enable me to find better answers for my most pressing ethical questions. I began to value college for what it could help me learn about myself and others, for what I could learn about art, music, literature, politics and science, and last and least, I'm afraid, for what a diploma could mean in the job market. I shall say a little more about what I think a college education should be, but now I would like to outline the personal experiences I had which made me begin to think for myself.

Until I had completed my freshman year in high school, my basic attitudes were not really in conflict with my parents' ideas. I believed in God, I went to church regularly, I believed what they told me about the wrongness of young people having sexual experiences prior to marriage. Since my parents are not very politically minded, I did not grow up with strong political preferences; but I did believe that the United States was always peace-loving, generous and altruistic.

The only thing I remember I disagreed with was my mother's assertion that I shouldn't see films that were not approved by the Legion of Decency. I would tell her that in the ones that I had seen I hadn't found anything objectionable. "That's just it," she would say, "you don't have enough experience to judge these things." She protested that these films were insidious in that they glamorized a false picture of life, giving the young viewer a distorted picture of reality. She felt, as I suppose the Legion did too, that the European films were the worst offenders, with their casual attitudes toward affairs, adultery, etc. Naturally I had no defense. When I was fifteen, I hadn't had any adult experiences and I did have to admit that the sort of life portrayed in the films *was* different from a high-school freshman's realm.

As an indication of how much my feelings have changed since I was a freshman, I should mention that though I never check the Legion's list, I suspect that I now rarely see any films which the Legion of Decency approves. It seems that the kind of film they like is a movie with a sugary, "nice" story, a story which has been emasculated of all the socially destructive or selfish human emotions, a story from which allusions to sexual desire, violence and crime have been pruned. To illustrate what I mean by a "nice" story, let me pick an easy target. I'm certain that I'm not the only one who read the Bobbsey Twins books when I was younger and thought that something was fishy about the twins' thoughtfulness of one another. Those stories never rang true because I had a younger brother with whom I fought regularly. If there was candy to share, I usually wondered how I might get more than my fair portion. Rare was the day that I ever volunteered to do housework beyond my assigned chores, and I might add that my brother was no better than I in these respects. If children are not downright selfish, they are in any case not aware of other people's needs and wants. If they are generous one day by doing a favor for someone, it is because the spontaneous impulse hit them that very day and they felt like doing it. The child doesn't do a kindness because he feels a sense of duty or because he knows he should be generous and thoughtful of others. We might think it would be nice if children strived to be, and always were, thoughtful, but children's minds do not work that way. The author of the Bobbsey Twins series may have gained a "nice" story in creating two sets of angelic twins, but he cheated honest human emotions by doing it. In much the same way, films like those approved by the Legion of Decency are innocuous, pleasant perhaps, but ultimately faulty portrayals of human beings.

When I was still in my early teens I had a crush on a girl who lived in our neighborhood. She was a cute girl, had lots of dates and was well liked. I was jealous of her attentions and admired her without qualification. It seemed to me that she was everything I wanted to be and wasn't; she had a nice figure and mine was still slightly boyish; she had boyfriends and dates and I had none; she was socially poised and I was awkward and insecure. I was always delighted to have her spend overnight with me and the two of us would usually talk until three or four in the morning. Once during one of our late bull sessions she confided that she had had relations with her boyfriend. Although I tried not to show it, I was really taken aback. How could someone I liked so much do something like that? Of course, I had heard the expression "It can happen to any girl," but I certainly never expected it to happen to this girl I idolized; and of course, I knew *I* would never do something like that. One of my basic attitudes had been challenged: a nice girl I knew had done the thing that only "bad" girls do and I had to find some satisfactory explanation for this experience of mine. I compromised. I thought less of her at the time—she had fallen in my eyes, although I still liked her immensely. However, I realized that it really *did* happen to some very nice girls. Even so, I thought I was more virtuous than she, since I hadn't had relations with a boy myself. (I have since learned the truth of a French saying that one who has never been tempted cannot call himself virtuous.)

It wasn't long before I had to do some more thinking along those lines. I was shy at that age and very insecure. I often doubted that I would ever fall in happily reciprocated love. I had crushes on several boys but none seemed to be interested in me. I would have given practically anything for an admiring male, and I soon gave everything I had when I found one. The man was a painting instructor at a local museum; he was thirtyish, unstable, and unhappily married. He had had too many affairs to count, was on his second marriage and was outwardly cynical. I initially felt for him a woman's fascination with, and affection for, a cynical man. I genuinely liked the art classes and was a good student, but I worked extra hard because I liked him and wanted to please him. I think he was touched by my naïve affection for him and we had an affair that lasted for about a year. I was sorry when it ended, but I had become a changed person: more mature, wiser and more self-confident. Although the man had given me false expectations, I never regretted our relationship or felt bitter toward him, because my experiences with him changed my life dramatically.

Virtually all my basic attitudes had to undergo scrutiny because of this relationship and I started to fashion my attitudes to fit my experience.

Naturally the first question that came up was the question of premarital sex. I have already mentioned what I thought of girls who had relations, and I found myself having them with a married man. Was I to condemn myself for behaving as I was or was I to change my opinion of girls who had affairs? I was unable to find a satisfactory answer to this dilemma for a couple of years and the resolution came only after I had restructured my whole concept of morality.

This man was the first who had offered me the affection and admiration that I sorely wanted and I was deeply attached to him. I frankly admitted to myself that I had no desire to end our relationship. Although I felt shame at this initial realization I started to get somewhere only by coming to terms with my actual feelings. It is a real surprise to discover that one harbors an unacceptable feeling. We all occasionally find that others do things we do not expect, that is, do or say something that seems incongruous with the image we have of them; but it comes as a much greater shock to find out something about oneself, something that doesn't fit one's self-image. When we thus surprise ourselves we may either repress or falsify our feelings to fit our self-image or we may admit that perhaps we didn't have an entirely realistic appraisal of ourselves in the first place. Well, I decided that my self-image of the good, chaste, religious girl evidently needed revamping. When I thought about it I realized that not only did I desire to continue to see this man even though the Church certainly frowned upon this relationship, but also that I did not even feel that I was especially bad for doing this. I was a good student in school and was doing some volunteer community work. No one knew about our affair and so I was not blatantly hurting someone else. I did feel guilty, but I couldn't feel that I was a totally bad person.

Taking honest stock of my feelings was the first step in resolving the quandary, but I still couldn't settle things right away. Actually, so long as this conflict between condemning myself or condoning premarital relations remained my most important moral conflict, I was not able to resolve things. I believe that we solve some conflicts and outgrow others. This conflict I outgrew. I was beginning to get beyond the conflict when I started to feel more accepting toward others. I began to think that whatever kind of relationship two consenting people wished to share was entirely their own business so long as others were not hurt. I became less judgmental, even toward those whose behavior I considered destructive, such as alcoholics, blackmailers and murderers. After a while I noticed that my concept of morality had changed its colors and shape. Qualities I had once considered important to a moral kind of person, such as being a churchgoer and following the sex mores of our culture, no longer seemed especially important. Rather, I began to think that consideration of, and love for one's fellow man was most important. That is why I now feel that a pacifist living with a woman, who takes a stand against what war does to his fellow man, can reach a higher state of moral consciousness than, say, a businessman who is married and faithful to his wife, yet never thinks about whether or not his nation has the right to inflict the cruelties it does against the miserable Viet Cong and their families. I think the college kid who doesn't go to church but who joins the Student Non-Violent Coordinating Committee and helps Negroes register in the South can be a more moral person than the realtor who attends church every Sunday but makes his money by helping to perpetuate ghetto conditions in racially mixed cities. As my ideas about morality changed, the conflict I had once experienced no longer seemed important. I had in a sense gotten beyond my problem; and with my different perspective, I no longer felt impelled to make a final judgment upon myself.

In every large city there are salvationists who walk the city streets literally shouting and screaming about how evil we all are and how soon judgment day is coming. When we see one of these people, we feel slightly embarrassed and uncomfortable; we wish to avoid their glances, and if we by chance take some of their literature, we feel we are humoring them. We may feel that they are well-intentioned but what they say seems to have little connection with our own lives. Far fewer people would attend church if they could only hear the kind of fire-and-brimstone sermon that a salvationist would give, for they would feel that sermons had little or no relevance to their daily lives. Fortunately, most churches have abandoned such kinds of preachings for sermons better suited to the needs of the congregation members.

Yet most churches still insist upon a rather restrictive code of behavior, sometimes forcing members to leave the congregation if they find that they personally do not wish to comply with the expected standards.

Of course, my affair posed a conflict with my church: I found that I could not be a member in spiritual good standing until I stopped seeing this man, renounced my behavior and felt contrite. I knew I certainly felt ambivalent and guilty, but I can't say I felt contrite. As there seemed to be no reconciliation with my church short of breaking off with the man, I avoided going to church for the time being. If at that time I had known a priest who had been interested in learning what my individual problems and needs were and who would have helped me to receive guidance even though I could not abide by the Church's rules just then, I might have remained a member of the Church. But the only advice I received was stock advice, the kind given to everyone regardless of his personal emotional make-up. I was advised to stop seeing this man and this was a request that I was not psychologically prepared to comply with at the time. I think I stopped going to church not only because I wanted to continue my affair, but also because I found that I was not getting the guidance I needed for the moral conflict I was experiencing. Just as the salvationist sermons do not seem to get to the heart of the things that concern us most, I could not find in the sermons at my church much that seemed to touch on the things that were most upon my mind.

It is regrettable but true that most churches fail to meet the guidance needs of many members of their congregations, especially young people. They fail partly because the codes of behavior that they insist upon are not flexible enough to allow for individual variation, and partly because in some instances, their codes are unrealistic. These churches will find that the members who fail to receive guidance that is vitally relevant to their lives will stop attending church and begin to search elsewhere for direction.

Although most churches still demand conformity with fairly rigid codes of behavior, some more progressive churches have attempted to both loosen up the existent standards to take into account the uniqueness of each member of the congregation and to revise or bring up to date the standards expected of church members. For example, there now is an interdenominational organization called the Council on Religion and Homosexuality, which is a group formed by churches who know that homosexual members of congregations are frequently driven away from church because of the church's attitudes against them. This group offers counseling and group therapy not with the intention of having homosexuals change their sexual orientation but rather with the intention of helping them to integrate their way of life with their religion. Sometimes clergymen who do much of their work with young people are very progressive, for they have learned the importance of preaching sermons which reflect knowledge and acceptance of the actual behavior of young people. For example, such a progressive clergyman knows that a sermon which acknowledges the commonness of premarital intimacies and then seeks to discuss how one can integrate this kind of behavior with the larger concerns of his religion will draw many more young listeners than one which in essence just scolds people for their behavior, telling them that such behavior is incompatible with their religion.

As I myself found that I didn't fit into my church, I began to look elsewhere for the answers to my moral problems. I became eager to learn about other people who had experienced similar conflicts, and I soon acquired a group of friends, some of whom were avowedly atheist. I began to worry about whether or not I believed in a supernatural being, and whether or not I could accept a belief in a heaven and hell. During my freshman year in college I took a biology course which was taught from the standpoint that there is a natural explanation for all the phenomena that one can encounter in the universe. The instructor was sympathetic with students who were trying to decide what they believed, for he had been raised by a Christian missionary and had himself experienced conflicts in his youth between his religious upbringing and scientific interests. I had several talks with the man and by the end of that term felt satisfied that one did not have to believe in a supernatural being in order to account for the creations of the universe. As the existence of a kind of paternal God who created the universe seemed more and more remote of a possibility to me, so did the existence of a heaven, hell or any kind of afterlife. As I had failed to receive the answers to my moral questions within the Church, and as I felt that I no longer believed in even the most basic teachings of my church, I stopped thinking of myself as a member.

I didn't reject the Church overnight or accept myself overnight either. One doesn't throw over a conventional moral upbringing right away. But during the year that I had the affair with this man and for two or three years afterward I found that the best way to have peace with myself was to follow my own intuitions and inclinations, carefully and thoughtfully molding my attitudes to the experiences I was having. I discovered that no one follows all the rules and that no one achieves an inner serenity by trying to be what others want him to be. Perhaps the most important lesson to come out of those years was the knowledge, hard won, that what I thought of myself was much more important than what I feared others thought of me. I found that so long as I considered myself a good person, worthy of respect, I actually was one.

Partly as a result of my affair I did not lead the usual kind of social life at high school. I was not much interested in the talk about boys, dates, how far to go on dates, dances and Elvis Presley. The boys did not interest me for they were too immature. I became a kind of outsider and found my only real compansionship with a small group of other outsiders. Together we comprised the "offbeat" element of my high school. We were mostly good students and a couple of teachers took some interest in us and helped us form a discussion group. At our meetings anything was game—economic policies, politics, religion, and the government, although it seemed that we mostly discussed politics and the government. We were encouraged to be aware of minority opinions as well as popular opinions on any issue, and all of us found that we occasionally sided with less popular stands on particular issues. All who participated in this group became better informed about Washington's affairs in general, but I think the main value of this group was that it exposed us to news sources other than the major newspapers, weekly magazines and major studio broadcasts. We discovered that some magazines such as *The Nation* and *New Republic* printed news that was not reported in the popular mass media, and we found a noncommercial educational radio station whose daily broadcasts were relatively unbiased and complete.

After I had entered college I took an English class in which the professor went a step beyond having the students seek out news sources besides the mass media. He encouraged us to read political magazines from foreign countries so that we might be more aware of what our actions looked like to other peoples and how our policies affected them. If nothing else, we learned from reading foreign journals that it is almost impossible for a country to be fair and impartial when its self-interests are involved in a conflict.

From the reading of a variety of journals of political opinion, including some foreign journals, one can gain a perspective, an ability to step back from the problems so that he can judge more clearly. It seems germane to mention that I think with very few (a really insignificant number) of exceptions, the people who write letters to Congress, to the White House and to newspapers expressing disapproval of U.S. policy are definitely not Communists or agents of foreign governments. They are simply citizens who have made themselves aware of how American policy looks to other nations. The Vietnam situation is a particularly good example because it has aroused more than average public interest, and the protesters of U.S. policy have been open and vocal. To somewhat oversimplify for the sake of example, it appears to Washington that Communists have infiltrated South Vietnam and are precluding fair elections from taking place. Yet it appears to almost every other nation, to many reliable U.S. political commentators and to the protesters that, at least before U.S. troops were sent, infiltration had not taken place to any considerable extent. These people feel that the Viet Cong movement grew indigenously; that it is indigenously supported; and that the U.S. intervention is therefore unwarranted and a violation of national sovereignty.

When one is aware of such conflicting opinions two questions come to mind. First, which account should one believe, and second, if one decides that his own country is in error, can he refuse to support its policy and remain a loyal citizen? In deciding which account of a situation sounds most realistic I generally consider the source. Does the person or agency giving this account have vested interests which may bias his perceptions? If you ask a laborer, a manager and an arbitrator to give you an outline of the issues of a labor dispute you will most likely get different stories from each one. I tend to rely upon accounts from sources who have the least number of interests in the situation. Also, I naturally have my favorite political commentators whose opinions I consider before I decide. Thirdly, I favor certain news agencies over others. I am highly suspicious, for example, of the news I find in popular magazines or hear over major network radio and television broadcasts. I don't trust the mass media altogether because economic considerations often pressure owners and advertisers into presenting the kind of news they think listeners will want to hear. If they fear that certain information may offend their public, this information is sometimes withheld or slanted. I recently read about an instance of such editorial censorship in a woman's magazine. The featured article was by a woman who had investigated a major network's refusal to sponsor a program dealing with teen-age venereal disease. The article explained that although the subject was potentially delicate, an infinite number of pains had been taken o make the program suitable for family viewing. The author cited quotations from the script showing it to be a model of good taste. Even the federal government had given its wholehearted approval to the project. Yet at the last minute, the network refused to sponsor the program saying that they felt it would not be appropriate material for all family viewing. The article concluded that a program which would have been of major value in educating the general public and especially teen-agers about a widespread health threat had, in effect, been dropped because the network and its advertisers were afraid of offending some of their audience.

Once one has examined an issue and has decided what to believe, he possibly faces the issue of loyalty. If he feels his country is wrong, can he refuse to support its policies and remain loyal? As I see it, individuals who do not support a policy entertained by Washington do so because they feel that the governmental course of action may be immediately indefensible, or harmful in the long run, or both. For instance, those who are against the U.S. presence in Vietnam are convinced that military intervention there is impractical, is a violation of a foreign power's national sovereignty, and will in the long run cause resentment toward the U.S. In other words, they believe that current policy is both inappropriate at present and will do future harm. With the good of the country in mind, these people want to see these policies changed and so they refuse to support current policy hoping to force a change for the better. By my lights, such a citizen is admirably loyal. He doesn't passively follow policy without regard for its future consequences. He tries to keep both the short- and long-range interests of his country in mind.

At this point I would like to say a couple of things about the kind of people who find that their conscience impels them to show disapproval of U.S. policies. I have already expressed my concern and dismay that the mass media often appear to be less reliable news sources than certain small independent magazines, newspapers and radio stations; I would add that I have also been consistently disappointed in the popular reporting of political demonstrations. The mass media have done a great disservice to a good many conscientious citizens by carelessly attaching lables which not only are usually inaccurate, not only have no relevance to the issues at hand, but also invite the public to misunderstand the intentions of the demonstrators. These people who have given their time (which is as precious to them as it is to anyone else) in order to wake up the public to a particular issue get laughed off in the press as only a bunch of beatniks, or worse yet, as Left-wingers if not actual Communists. Many a person who reads the article wondering what the march was all about reads until he sees the phrase "Left-wing," "Socialist" or "Communist" and then subconsciously closes his mind. All he knows is that Left-wingers are bad and that the demonstrators must be proposing something subversive if they are Left-wing. When he encounters the magic phrases two things happen: he ignores the issue that the demonstrators had wished to make him aware of, and he forms a bad opinion of the demonstrators and their cause. No doubt, there are a few Communists here and there (though I have never met any) and a handful of Left-wingers who participate in these demonstrations, but I don't think these leftists are usually in charge. The bulk of demonstrators, I believe, are people like those I know personally: students and others who have no special love for Communism, Socialism or any other "ism." They are people who just think that someone—maybe a minority group in this country, maybe the citizens of a foreign country—is not getting a fair deal.

These people who have stuck up for someone's human rights are severely disappointed when they read accounts in local newspapers of a demonstration in which they have participated that sometimes outright, most often by devious implication, suggests that the movement was Communist-led or Communist-infiltrated. They know exactly how the public will react to a write-up that makes them appear to be political subversives. It is a real letdown to know that because of unfair reporting, the cause which they had genuinely hoped would get public recognition may actually be damaged instead. It is little wonder that some of these young idealists either grow sour toward the system that misjudged their intentions or else adopt an "I don't care any more" attitude.

As you might expect, the relatonship I had with my parents underwent some strains as my outlook began to change from so many different angles. It is hard for a young person to live with his parents after he first decides they are not always right. He doesn't want to hurt or offend them, yet if he fails to make his own unique adjustment to adulthood, he remains psychologically dependent upon them. By the time I had entered college, my differences with my parents had become considerable, and although they usually granted me much more freedom to be myself than most of my classmates' parents, I moved away so that the differences would not be so painful. For the last year or so of high school and for the first couple of years of college, I had very little communication with my parents beyond newsy trivia. I think it is fairly typical for young people to seek distance from their parents for several years. Until he has found a satisfactory outlook that is comfortable and is his own, the young person feels threatened by his parents' views. He wants to experience the world in terms of his unique emerging self; he does not want to experience life from his parents' viewpoint. It is all right to see from Daddy's shoulders when you're little, but one must eventually grow tall enough so he can see for himself. The young person almost instinctively knows, if he does not suffer psychological handicaps, that he will grow best without parental help or interference. During this period of growth the young individual walls himself off from serious communication with his parents so that his adult self can begin to take shape.

During the last couple of years my parents and I have become good friends, able to communicate with each other better than ever. When we began to talk seriously again I found that they too had changed a lot since when I was younger. I have a new kind of respect for them and they are able to respect me for what I am and for the way I conduct my life, even though they would probably not live their lives as I have mine had they a second chance.

Now that I have outlined the experiences that changed my whole outlook I come once again to the question of education and what it means for me. Although I have discussed how I arrived at my feelings about religion, morality and politics from a highly personal standpoint, other college students have formed their personal outlook in similar ways. They too have undergone the bewildering but treasured set of social and academic experiences which result in a new image of themselves, a college diploma, and the beginning of a lifelong search directed toward developing ever more acute and sensitive sight. Though I intend to speak only for myself, I suspect my idea of what an education should be will be shared by many other students like me.

To begin negatively, college is not just, or even primarily, an academic experience. To my mind someone who graduates and doesn't just *feel* different has missed a lot. He may know more about his field, but if he doesn't also know much more about himself it is as if he only got to the soup and missed the entree and dessert altogether. It's a little harder to specify just what an education is if it isn't primarily academic, but I'll try my best to describe the general feel of it. It has to do with that period of growth, that adjustment to adulthood. In immediate human terms, the period of growth makes more difference in the final product than does the refinement of academic learning. Of course, academics plays a part, and an important one. I frankly can't imagine how I would have arrived at the personal outlook I have today had I not had the chance to learn some college science, to step outside our own culture and time through literature and the humanities, and to learn more about our contemporary world through the social sciences. But balanced against these academic experiences were the times I had very honest personal talks with professors outside class, the times another student and I were able to get rid of defenses for a while and really communicate. It was mostly at these intimate times that I was willing to test my beliefs to see if they really fit. Fortunately, I don't have to decide whether I would rather have missed the academic or the social experiences that together are part of an education. They work well in combination and not very well at all separately. I want only to say that one misses a great deal if he goes to college only for academic reasons.

But thus far I have only sketched an abstract shadow of what the student looks like who is integrating all the experiences available to him and making them a part of himself. To get a feel for him you must know what he concretely looks like. To begin with, I should say that his religious faith takes a serious battering, and is more often than not shattered. There are atheists and agnostics on almost any campus and many campuses have only a minority of students claiming a specific faith. I don't think I can count the times that I have overheard while having lunch a conversation from a nearby table between a couple of people hashing over their thoughts on religion. It's always a hot issue on campus regardless of one's personal feelings. And the fact that more and more students find that they personally cannot abide by religion as it has been traditionally understood suggests to me that our whole society, not just a few theologians, is going to have to do some new thinking in this area.

The "full" student is almost certain to change his ideas about premarital sex, for even if he has no experiences himself (a possibility increasingly unlikely) he will certainly have close friends who do. Just as he should have flirted with atheism, he would do well to try free love for a while. He may try consciousness-expanding drugs to stretch the range of his experience, and he may become a Socialist (but rarely a Communist). Because there will be a gap left if he rejects his religion, he may become interested in Zen or humanism in order to fill it. As he finds out more about other countries he may decide that the U.S. is not necessarily the kindest to its own citizens, or necessarily the most altruistic. He may grow to dislike business. And as all these peripheral changes are taking place, he will incidentally learn something about his field of study.

For those readers who feel rather aghast at these things that will happen in college—and they *will* to *most* sensitive, searching young people—there is fortunately a gain which more than redresses anything lost, though it is fairly intangible. But even though this gain is intangible I shall try to describe it as meaningfully as I can.

As a result of shattering some, modifying other, and adopting new beliefs, one begins to know himself better. He has tried on many different kinds of beliefs and has chosen the ones that for the time being fit best. When one finds he must change his outlook in this way or that, he becomes both more critical and more open-minded. One is not taught how to be critical in schools; he is not taught how to judge whether or not a movie is a realistic portrayal of human behavior or how to determine whether or not a politician is really saying anything new behind the mask of words. One becomes critical when he becomes more sensitively sighted as a result of having had to examine his own beliefs and behavior.

One generally finds that a sensitive self-examination leads to a better understanding of others and their particular problems. One day I was driving behind a car with a bumper sticker that read "I'm Fighting Poverty—I'm Working." I assumed that the driver of that car probably did not understand very well the problems of those people at whom the anti-poverty program is directed. I imagine he was judging the situation in terms of his own experience. He had probably never had a problem finding work because he was white and his educational background was probably sufficient for good work. How natural for him to suppose that anyone out of work was really just lazy! Making such judgments about others in terms of personal experience is harder to do after one's beliefs have once had a good shaking up. This is partly because one is a little more receptive and interested in others' problems since he feels that he may learn from others in solving his own conflicts; and it is also partly because he knows that he once made his judgments from a standpoint which later proved to be inappropriate, and he perhaps wishes to avoid judging someone else by inappropriate standards.

I think by and large people who have revised their outlooks are a little more generous and accepting of others. After all, who knows better than they how fallible human judgments are about people, things and events. The first time I saw a film by Michelangelo Antonioni, I felt cheated. I had paid two dollars to see what seemed to me a pointless study of the blasé Italian upper classes. Sometime later after I had changed in many ways, I saw another of his films dealing with the same ennui. I was more accepting. I found that the film did have a point, although it didn't hit especially close to home with me. With my more generous eyes I saw that Antonioni is really a skilled director and that his work deserves praise. I wasn't so quick to conclude that if I personally didn't become involved in the film the failing was in the artistic achievement.

In the movie *Room at the Top* there is a character named Alice who is played by Simone Signoret. Alice is a wise, kind and gentle person who is a good listener and who understands and brings out the best in the male lead character, Joe. One cannot help but admire this magnificent woman who because she has the gift of allowing people to be what they are helps Joe to become more human. Alice has an affair with Joe which is not much of a secret from the small town where they both work, and at one point, one of the residents refers to Alice as "that old whore." When I was viewing the film my reaction to that epithet was "How inappropriate!" It would never have occurred to me to stick Alice, the wonderful humanitarian who in her womanly fashion got right to Joe's inner core, in this category. Alice was a real human being who transcended all such categories. The phrase "an old whore" has a bad connotation and describes a certain set of characteristics: an older woman, one who allows many men to know her. But this set of characteristics really says nothing about the kind of person who may fall within the limitations of the characteristics. Alice was in her forties and had known men other than her husband and Joe. But Alice was much, much more: she was a natural psychologist and a woman full of undemanding love. Alice was being sold short by being shoved into that derogatory category.

We all think categorically and find this kind of thinking a prerequisite to mental order. But we must be willing quickly to relinquish categories and stereotypes if they are not appropriate. And we must always realize that whenever we put a person into a category we are selling him short. My education has toned down my own rigid thinking, and that is a gain which takes care of all other possible losses all by itself. Never can I personally be quite so categorical as I was when I was fifteen, nor can anyone else whose beliefs have been once revamped.

What I call my education has been a very total experience. I think differently, I *feel* different all over and I even look different from the person I was before, and I am not sorry for the changes.

The New Reality

PHILO B. BAUMGARTNER*

1

INFANCY, the original condition of human existence, is a state of total relatedness within a small but complete universe. When the newborn child is held in his mother's arms, welded to her body and taking nourishment from her breast, his whole being is bathed in an environment of unconditional acceptance and nurturing. Every fiber of his nervous system, every ounce of his being is in total ecstasy, a singular ecstasy that our language clumsily, grossly divides up into such concepts as "love," "sexuality," "hunger," "gratification." The quality of this infantile ecstasy is comparable to the moments of mystical ecstasy or of the ecstasy of love between two people that we adults rarely, if ever, experience to our fullest capacity.

This ecstatic union of infant and mother is traumatically shattered if she separates herself from him at a stage in his biological-emotional development when his nervous system is still incomplete without her. Through a combination of forced weaning and imposed isolation, which are so much a part of our culture's child-rearing practices, the infant is periodically separated from not only his physical life source (mother's breast), but also his emotional life source (mother's arms and reassuring voice). Isolated in his crib at night, and for long hours

* *Philo Baumgartner, age twenty-eight, is the son of a career officer in the U. S. Army. Since completing his two years of military service and being honorably discharged, he has worked as a counselor in various summer and day camps, including the Boy Scouts. Currently a graduate student in the Department of Speech, he plans to teach in a progressive private school, preferably Quaker.*

during the day, he is deprived of the love that he so profoundly and continuously needs. Two things then happen to him simultaneously: first, the ecstasy of complete union with the all-important object of love and source of nourishment is interrupted; the infant's nervous system is left isolated; and second, the baby's world has been divided into two parts, the "inner" and the "outer." He becomes aware that there is an external reality, his mother, upon whom his internal cosmos of physical and emotional fulfillment is totally dependent.

Now a fragmented, incomplete creature, his whole being yearns for the re-establishment of his former completeness. Mother is outside his cosmology now, and he can only get her back at arbitrary moments, and by adopting certain poses. Although he hasn't yet learned the words for it, he learns that "good little boys don't cry," that is "good little boys" repress their intense yearning for completeness, for unconditional gratification and love. This repression of crying is an unconscious reflex conditioning. Without being aware of it, he is being conditioned to be the child that mother expects and wants him to be in order that he will be allowed to relate his feelings to this most important of other human beings, to be held in her arms, receive affection, and be fed. Mother's expectations form the concept that the child has of who and what he is; they are the beginnings of a social reality that the child is forced to accept, a social reality that distracts him from direct, intimate relatedness, alienating standards of behavior and artificial goals of achievement. Meeting the demands of a social reality that becomes increasingly complex, and which demands more and more of his life energies as he grows older, is a vicious circle that cuts deeper and deeper into the part of him that is most vital, spontaneous, and creative. In order to attain fulfillment, he must meet the parental and societal expectations that are conditions for this fulfillment. In order to meet these expectations, he must increasingly repress his own inner impulses, including the impulses of affection and creativity as well as his destructive impulses.

In our culture, strict toilet training is often imposed on the infant before he has had a chance to develop spontaneous control over his bowels. He is conditioned, by punishment and withdrawal of affection and approval, to eliminate according to an artificial schedule, rather than according to the natural, uninhibited cycle of his own needs.

This conditioning, this imposition of an order alien to his own bodily functions, becomes deeply ingrained in his nervous and muscular systems, and carries over into his personality. He grows into a compulsive, deeply inhibited adult who is unable to freely "let go" and express his feelings. His own conditioned nervous system becomes the chains that will hold him in physical and emotional captivity. His own body comes to be experienced as an external, alien "thing." When he reaches adulthood, his physical movements will be wooden and expressionless. He will feel separated from the world he is in, unable to touch freely, and feeling, in turn, untouchable. In his emotional as well as physical untouchability and isolation, he will be unable to allow a free flow of intimate contact and mutuality between himself and others. Conditioned to fulfill strict, unrealistic demands, he strives for a nonhuman perfection that blinds him to the full humanness both of himself and others.

He is further limited in his contact with others and with the physical world around him by our own particular culture's sanctions against free sensory exploration and expression. We've all heard parents say to their children, "Don't ever touch Daddy's tools again; you'll break them," or "Don't pet that strange dog, he's filthy, and he probably has some kind of nasty disease," or "Don't touch that man's car; that's his private property," or "It's very bad to look at Suzy when she's undressed." This is systematic, often vengeful deprivation of direct sensory experience. The world becomes full of tantalizing, forbidden objects that cannot be lived directly, but must be handled at arm's length by the unwieldly, unfeeling tongs of mental concepts. As children we learn that there is such a thing as "sex." We learn this not through what we experience directly, but rather through what we *don't* directly experience. Our awareness of sex is based on a conglomeration of peer group tall tales, medical explanations, half-truths hinted at by hedging parents, and the teasing myths presented by Hollywood, cheap novels, burlesque shows, and girlie magazines. "Dirt" of any kind becomes an object of repulsion because of our conditioning; yet it is at the same time an object of fascination for the very reason that it represents those parts of our personal experiences that our culture refuses to acknowledge.

In grasping the conceptual meaning of an experience and missing its quality and feeling, we handle the world with the arid structures of a priori attitudes, but deny the same right to our senses. A child senses and responds directly to anger in another person, even though he is unaware of what the concept "anger" means, why the person is angry, or what he is angry at. The adult tends to be blind to an emotion in himself or in another person unless he can put a name to it, fit it into a culturally recognized category, or establish "reasons" for the existence of the emotion. Often we misapply conceptions about emotions to actual emotions and confuse the actuality of a series of emotional responses with what we have defined this series of responses to signify. As I start to walk across a narrow log that spans a deep ravine, adrenaline pours through my system; I am keyed up and slightly trembling; my mouth is dry. What I experience is simply a state of excitement, heightened nervous alertness, muscular readiness, and strength needed to accomplish this difficult task. However, my mind goes one step beyond the immediate circumstances, misinterprets what is simply a physical state of excitement, and labels it "fear." This means, then, that "I'm afraid to walk across the log," with the result that I back off of it.

I don't know just how it has come about, but in America we have evolved what is perhaps one of the most schizophrenic cultures in the history of mankind. Seldom has a way of life so misrepresented and distorted the nature of human feeling and the objects of human needs and desires as does ours. I am speaking of emotional wants and needs rather than strictly physical subsistence requirements such as food and shelter. We don't seem to be so hung up in symbols about food, for example, as we are in symbols about sex. When we're hungry, we don't just stand in front of a billboard and salivate at a picture of food as if the picture *were* food; we go directly for food, whether we find a restaurant and eat, cook our own meal, or stand on a corner and beg for food. On the other hand, I've seen countless numbers of men, including myself, leafing through girlie magazines, drooling at pictorial representations of sexual delight as if the objects of desire had existence on the printed page. The conceptualization of "sex" has isolated an inherent, inseparable quality in human relationships and plastered it on billboards, in magazines, movie screens, and burlesque shows, and we, poor male victims, salivate like Pavlov's misdirected dogs. It has taken me a long time to realize that when I am attracted to the shapes of a woman's breasts, hips, and buttocks, I am being caught up in a collection of *ideas* about sexuality; I am responding more to a well-filled sweater than to an actual human female.

As we take on the social roles of "son," "schoolmate," "athletic star," "employee," "husband," "father," "club member," "drinking associate," or "churchgoer," we form a public personality, and our private inner self dwindles, clamoring ever more hopelessly for recognition not only from others, but from ourselves as well. In the eyes of those who are most dear to us we are expected to be "somebody," or "something" other than who or what we are. They love this "somebody," leaving the central core of our being lonely, unrecognized, unfulfilled. We all do this to one another, not callously or uncaringly, but ignorantly, unable to stop it. Not only are we left alone, but the huge lust for life that we all contain glowers like banked coals inside of us, mute and ineffective, yet potentially explosive, seeking an outlet that may or may not be destructive, depending on the amount and intensity of our frustration.

A child is subtly, constantly, often unintentionally, reminded that he is a little "nobody" who might become a big "somebody" if he "grows up" and realizes certain cultural goals. The realm of social reality and expectation hits a child exceptionally hard when he's about nine, ten or eleven years old. He isn't free to enjoy playing baseball just for the sheer enjoyment of it; he is too busy being concerned about winning, or being a star player. A couple of summers ago I worked in a day camp with nine- and ten-year-old boys. When they played games, especially such culturally honored games as baseball and football, the pressure of competition, the need to win, was often an intolerable strain on them. Boys from the losing team would come into the building, their eyes streaming bitter tears of defeat. They literally sobbed with rage and frustration. It was immediately obvious which was the losing team, so that I didn't have to ask "Who won?"; I asked instead, "Was it a good game? Did you enjoy it?" They looked at me as though I were crazy, as if enjoyment were the furthest thing from their minds. To them, playing baseball wasn't just a game; it was life and death; and to lose a game meant to die, at least for a little while.

To a boy of this age "communication" doesn't mean the fulfillment of a desire for communion with a person he enjoys being with. It means a dialogue of rivalry covered up by a friendliness based on expediency. Or it means a word of approval from a prestigious peer.

When this grim little boy who rarely smiles with spontaneous delight becomes what we term an adult, the all-important conceptual world of his childhood changes into still another all-important and even more encapsulating conceptual world. From childhood he has come a long way; he no longer recognizes vague inner desires to do or be something different from what he has already committed himself to do or be. He has "matured"; that is, he now unquestioningly experiences himself entirely in terms of what the culture's symbols tell him that he is, needs, and desires. He is now a full-grown laboratory rat running through a social maze. He is hungry, and jumps through a door marked "food," or "love," or "friendship," and instead of food, or love, or friendship, he finds himself in a hall of distorted mirrors. He becomes so confused that he no longer knows if he's hungry, horny, lonely, or what. He has a vague, disruptive empty feeling that he tags "lonely." He feels that all he needs is companionship. However, he demands something other than the mere presence of the person he calls "friend." He demands of this person a verification of his own validity as a human being. He uses other people as mirrors to reflect back to himself an image of himself as he would like to be, but fears he isn't. He looks to others for this sought-after image of himself, because he fears that if he looked inside himself he would encounter, at best, a sense of personal unreality. When he encounters rejection from a person whose opinions, evaluations and expectations he values, he has looked into a mirror and has discovered "the horrible truth" about himself. Even when he receives the approval that he feels he needs, he has a vague subconscious feeling that he has been cheated; he is still lonely, because he has come in contact not with another human being, but merely another reflected version of his own self-image.

Sometimes people get to a point of despair in which they lose all hope of being reassured that they are what they "ought" to be. The very ideals that they identify with most strongly are a rejection of their own personal validity. These are people who feel a personal disintegration, yet cling to the very tools of their self-destruction. A homosexual bar is a very sad place, where dreams are stale, and the conversation, although lively at times, has the tone of inevitable disillusionment. The homosexual believes in an exaggerated, caricatured image of "masculinity," yet is convinced that he can identify with it only by putting himself in a subservient, humiliating position before it.

To dull the vicious cutting-edge of self-hate, a Negro sits in his ghetto apartment watching his TV. His mind glazed by liquor, he fantasizes, identifies with, and hopelessly yearns for a white world that is blinded to his existence by his color.

An alcoholic is an idealist who has been led to believe, or has led himself to believe, that he has a character flaw that prevents him from realizing his dreams of success. His awareness dulled by alcohol, he scarcely notices his surroundings; he dwells in a future that he is convinced will never materialize, or in a past full of failure and regrets. He is unable to change because he is caught in the grip of a time continuum, a mental dimension that extends from the "past" to the "future." He dwells in the twin realms of dead memories and unmaterialized possibilities. Reliving a past that he can never change, although his mental energies are directed at this hopeless task, and living in a future that he can't manipulate in his own mind because it isn't a reality in the present, he is blind to the only time that he can effectively take action in: the immediate here-and-now.

Isolated from his own senses, the frustrated person has only two alternatives. He can try to "explain" to himself what is happening, which only serves to support the cultural illusion that there is a "meaning" to actions and feelings that is detached from the senses. Or he can regress, and without giving in return, demand that the world give him what he wants or needs. This regression, which I see so much of in many members of the so-called "hip" generation, is a futile, impotent crying out for mother's breast, a reality that once was, but is now gone forever. There is only one way out of this dilemma: the creation of a new emotional climate, a new reality.

2

There are three realms of human existence, and they are all created by the nervous systems of individual human beings. There is the realm of dream, vision, mystic joy, love, ecstatic fulfillment and union, supreme universal harmony and order. There is the realm of infantile nightmare, loneliness, despair, abject terror, hatred, and universal chaos and destruction. And there is the realm of man's social reality; the reality of institutions, buildings and streets, families and business organizations, law and law enforcers, and churches and bars. The realms of dream and nightmare, which are so closely and inextricably intertwined in the human nervous system, have been partially institutionalized in the realm of social reality. Man has created both God and the Devil in his own images; the dream and the nightmare. One way to discover what man is, is to examine the God he has imagined. God can create a world out of meaningless flux; so can man. It was God's true identity, man, who expelled Adam, i.e., himself, from the Garden of Eden by eating of the fruit of self-consciousness. He became aware of his own nakedness; but first, he learned shame. He learned to want more than what was immediately at hand, and so created power. The use of this power, the concern over having this power, was what alienated him from the world he was born into; the Garden of Eden. The glory of God is simply man touching the naked body of his own dreams, and envisioning the Eden that is always at hand, and within the grasp of every human being.

Like God's counterpart, the Devil, man can also create a world of misery, terror, and perpetual hatred and revenge. Since our nervous systems have created all three realms, we are not inevitably committed to any one; salvation is not inevitable (we can see this in the child who futilely wails for love); neither is damnation inevitable; and neither is the limbo of utilitarian social reality.

In a sense, the entire world that we see and grasp with our minds is a creation of our own minds, nervous systems and viscera. We look at grass and see the color green in it. This is an illusion, because "green" is something that happens in our sense receptors, not in the grass. However, it serves our purposes to see "green" not as a state of mind, but as a quality "out there," inherent in the grass, even though it exists beyond our vision. The world is an inconceivable flux of nameless stuff and motion, which we term "atoms," "molecules," and "energy." However, we couldn't function if our nervous systems and brains didn't create some sort of order out of all this flux. The way we divide the world up into "things," "events," etc., is inherent in the way we think, but it isn't inherent in the way the world functions, or even in the way other people think. Our culture often takes this abstracting function of the human mind to such extremes that we divide up and combine people much to the detriment of human survival. I see an individual with dark skin, and classify him as "Negro"; that is, I *make* him a Negro in my own mind, although in actuality he is simply an individual human being.

Our culture, unlike many so-called "primitive" cultures, abstracts out of all the unclassifiable flux of experience, one and only one reality, any deviation from which is considered "fantasy," i.e., "unreal." We forget that what we call "fantasy" is created by the same imagination that creates what is culturally acceptable as "reality." Let me use a personal example: sometimes I prowl through the streets of my neighborhood like a cop on the beat, my senses wide open, exploring every doorway, savoring every nuance of shadow, lightness, darkness, speckling colors, stony or wooden or plastic or metal textures. Imagination and reality blend in my mind in a wide-awake dream. My neighborhood, which is just a collection of ordinary city streets, Victorian-style houses, bars, barber shops and restaurants, becomes enchanted. A city park, which is at the end of Haight Street, becomes the beginning of a forest. The streets are patched and worn, and have the undulating contours of a storybook road. A bar I go into has the faint, invisible flavor of a mythical caravansary, or of places like Samarkand, Bokhara, Baghdad. The plate-glass windows of restaurants are frosted over, giving them a faint flavor of Charles Dickens' London. It is almost dark, and the acid of a setting sun etches clear outlines of opaque clouds piling atop one another. There is a rawness in the air that sweeps away the city smell and leaves the street wide open as if it were a small town, a small community of lights in some vast Canadian wilderness.

My neighborhood, like any event, place, person, or thing, is an enigma. When we are busy working, studying, taking examinations, talking with people at a bar, driving a car, cooking a meal, or playing golf, we become very sure of what things are. There is no enigma, no infinite possibilities of what a thing could be; we say, "Reality is reality, and fantasy is fantasy." Imagination is not considered a part of the "real" world. What we call "reality" is a limitation of awareness to a single level out of all the possible levels of awareness that the mind is capable of. What we mean by "reality" is a strictly utilitarian awareness; a chair is nothing but a chair, and its sole purpose, its sole meaning is "sitting." "Reality" is also the realm of concepts and symbols which we live by in our daily lives; there are "laws" which make it morally obligatory not to cross a street against a red light; Lyndon B. Johnson is more than a mere person, he is also a sacred institution—"President" of the "United States of America"; people behave the way they do because they have "egos," or "ids"; the country operates in terms of "economic" or "political" "principles." Our everyday lives are filled with such mental creations as "laws," "morally obligatory," "President," "United States of America," "egos," "ids," "economic principles" and "political principles" which we accept as being the inevitable furniture of "reality," and which distract our attention from our own unique, personal mental creations. These latter are not included in society's inventory.

To view an object, person, or event as enigmatic is to affirm the infinity of possibilities that this object, person, or event could be. It is a realization that our cultural-linguistic "realities" are no more real, and need be no more binding upon us, than what we would *like* to be real. If the mind creates reality, why must it be in conformity with certain standard cultural rules? If I can function well enough to walk on sidewalks instead of the middle of the street, cross the street and avoid being hit by a car, walk into a restaurant and order a meal, go to work and perform all of my tasks, and successfully communicate with my fellow human beings, whether they be truck drivers, cops, professors, or artists, then why can't I create a reality for myself which has all the possibilities, all the rich, subtle, soul-satisfying flavors of a dream? If dreams are meaningful and beautiful beyond our experiences of ordinary utilitarian "reality," why not infuse ordinary "reality" with the beauty and desirability of dreams, and thereby create a reality that is more beautiful, more satisfying to my nervous system than the everyday "reality" my awareness is so often limited to? In the morning when I awake, I unwind myself from sleep and dreams. Still clinging to my mind are traces of long, lonely, sweet moments, of incredibly blue, vivacious oceans, foaming with the living foam of oceans painted by Japanese Zen masters. Still clinging to my senses are traces of the unfathomable depths of a woman's ardor, her infinitely soft lips and caressing limbs. Sometimes a day will be started by these dreams, and as the day unfolds, I will seek the reality of these dreams, in the air around me, in the faces of people I meet. There are occasions when I have experienced a union of dream and actuality. I have held a woman in my arms, and have felt deepening, growing ardor swelling like a cosmic sob in our welded bodies, just as with the unnamed woman in my dreams.

"Reality" to me implies a rigorous yet very subjective empiricism. That which is most immediately apparent to my nervous system, without the aid of deceiving drugs, is most "real" to me. My inner emotions cease to be idle fantasies that operate independently of the external world of people and things when I focus all of my attention on the immediate here-and-now. When I recognize that this moment of "now" and this place of "here" is the only moment and place that has valid existence for me, I bring internal "desire" and external fulfillment together. It is impossible to go back to infantile union with mother; it belongs to the realm of the dead past. It is possible to achieve union with the immediate here-and-now. This is not easy, and takes rigorous self-discipline. It is all too easy to postpone living for the "future"; to say "it'll happen tomorrow." When "tomorrow" becomes now, there is always another "tomorrow"; it is too easy to fall into the cultural habit of planning a future way of living, and keeping the here-and-now at arm's length. "Now" is the only part of our lives that is valuable; it is the only part of our lives that we are able to do anything in. Things don't come in neat packages in the immediate here-and-now; everything has the quality of enigma. Enigma is the point at which dream and fact meet; it is the point at which conventional meanings disintegrate and the pieces of experience can rearrange themselves into different meanings.

A moment of here-and-now is experienced with varying degrees of sharpness and clarity. I experienced one of the clearest, sharpest, most intense moments of my existence when I went on a camping trip down in Big Sur. I was with a couple of friends. We hiked along a stream until we came to a pool. At one end of the pool was a waterfall. We took off our clothes, jumped into the pool and waded over to it. We took turns walking into the waterfall. When I walked into it, the coldness of the water, the force of it pummeling my body violently obliterated all cerebral activities in my mind. For several seconds, my entire nervous system seemed to stand on end. I was cold but not "cold"; there was the physical sensation of coldness, but "coldness" didn't mean anything to me; it had neither pleasant nor unpleasant connotations. When I left the waterfall, my mind was purged from me, and I was simply a healthy, unthinking animal, all eyes, ears, and nerve endings. "Death," "pain," "happiness" didn't have any meaning for me; I was incapable of conceptualizing. From that moment on, the world around me was filled with exciting possibilities; I was ready to accept anything.

I would like to quote from Rollo May's collection of essays, *Existential Psychology,* two interesting examples of the same sort of total existence in the moment that I have just related:

> . . . a number of psychoanalysts are of the opinion that one of the main reasons that shock measures produce positive effects in patients is that these treatments provide them with a kind of death-and-rebirth fantasy experience.[1]

The shock treatment experience cuts the patient off from the time continuum of expectation, regret, and dread so that he is totally in the moment of his "rebirth"; he is a new person with no painfully reconstructed and re-enacted past, and no dreaded future.

> In some studies of pilots during World War II, it was found that those who did not break down psychologically retained, in the moments of most extreme danger, the illusion of invulnerability.[2]

This I interpret as the power of courage to bring the individual so immediately in contact with the here-and-now that all expectation or possibility of death is wiped out. The moment of existence, the moment of being so obviously alive, is so intense that the fiction of an anticipated futurity existing in the present is temporarily suspended.

As I live completely as I can in the here-and-now, I find myself

[1] Rollo May, ed., *Existential Psychology,* New York, Random House, 1961, p. 63.

[2] *Ibid.,* pp. 73–74.

very readily responding to people, things, and situations in a manner that is directly sensual. Little children and dogs are attracted to me. It's as easy for me to dance to music as it is to listen to it. However, it becomes increasingly difficult for me to think abstractly. When I meet a woman to whom I am attracted, I have an immediate desire to make contact. Social contact through a "meeting of minds" is difficult; I only want to look at her and satisfy my sense of sight; I want to listen not to her ideas, but to her voice, which expresses the way she feels; I want to touch her and feel the quality of her flesh, and the vitality of her life in that flesh; I want to dance with her and satisfy my desire for communication through movement. It's not necessarily "sex" that I'm after, but simply intimate, direct communication.

Staying away from the moment, putting living off until "tomorrow," is a way of avoiding the mysteries of blood, of life and death. It is a habitual postponement that adds on layers of fear, and more fear, to an experience that can stimulate at the most, a limited physical fear. Soon we get to the point of fearing even life itself. The fear of life becomes inseparable from the fear of death; indeed, they are one and the same. Whenever I anticipate orgiastic union with a woman, I anticipate violence. I'm not sure why, but I believe that it is a pretty universal feeling. Whenever I am deeply, emotionally, sensually moved by a woman, I sense some imaginary foe nearby who will challenge me, and whom I will have to fight with to the death. This insight into myself reminds me very much of Freud and his Oedipus complex. But this doesn't apply to my feeling exactly. The son fighting the father for the affections of mother may have been some sort of truth at one time in my life, but in my adult life, it is simply an allegory. "Woman" to me means not womblike security, but ecstasy and danger. The lion is out of the cage, but instead of rampaging about, he stands warily and cautious in his unexpected freedom, anticipating swift retribution for his state of freedom. Retribution is in the very air he sniffs, but he can't tell where it'll come from. The hidden foe is the self-punishing conditioning that sees ecstasy as a threat to the social order that I have been conditioned to accept. This foe is not an all-powerful "father," but a challenger who is on equal terms with me; I have at least as much a chance to defeat it as it has to defeat me.

This foe is in me, and its usual guise is an ugly thing called "habit." Habit isn't just a repetitive cycle of behavior; it is a deadly state of nonbeing, a self-putting down. Alcoholism isn't just getting drunk all the time; it is a state of self-imposed impotence that increasingly cuts a person off from fulfillment. His dreams and visions are no longer guides for action; they become a separate, unactualized, schizophrenic realm of life. Habit reinforces the illusion of a barrier between myself and other people, the illusion that my emotional needs are hopelessly imprisoned within myself, unable to escape. Habit keeps me away from having to face the "real nitty-gritty," but it leaves me unsatisfied. It is a foe that wears many mundane disguises, most of which I am finally catching onto. This one big life-denying habit, although I can't give a name to it since it exists deep within my nervous system and only shows itself in mental images of futility, alienation, personal inferiority, etc., lives in all of us. It is like a live creature in that it has no purpose but simply to survive. Childhood circumstances gave it birth, but it continues to survive long after these childhood circumstances are left in the dead past. The only way to stop thinking poorly of myself, and to stop failing consistently to accomplish the tasks that I consider important, is to stop nourishing this habit, to cut off all the specific, little day-to-day habits that support it.

When I was writing this paper, I got bogged down because I felt that I had nothing to say. This was the restricting self-image that I had, and I went through a self-defeating habit cycle that reinforced this self-concept. I would go to a bar at night, drink until closing time, then stagger home to bed. I'd wake up in the morning tired and hung over, decided "to hell with it," roll over, and go back to sleep. Waking up around noon or later, I realized that I hadn't accomplished anything, and therefore *couldn't* accomplish anything for the rest of the day. This self-defeating cycle went on for about a month until I decided that the only way I could produce was by breaking this cycle. One morning I woke up, hung over and tired as usual, and mentally kicked myself out of bed. I staggered bleary-eyed to the shower, washed myself awake, and managed to make it to class on time. During the whole time that I was breaking my sleep-in escapist habit pattern, whole sequences of ideas were being spontaneously formed in my hung over, rudely awakened mind; entirely new perspectives were being formed; perspectives that had never occurred to me previously. I realized that the simple act of breaking an old habit pattern represented an entirely new way of behaving, and evoked an entirely new outlook on life.

Since the time that I broke my drinking, sleeping-in, doing-nothing habit, I have added depth and meaning to my newly discovered outlook on life. I have stopped responding to the social chatter that passes for human communication. I exist in a silence that denies the existence of anything which I don't feel, physically or emotionally. I don't seek in others guides for the regulation of my thoughts and emotions. I don't look for anything in other people, because whatever I hope to find is already there in the immediate situation, and doesn't *need* to be searched for.

What I most need to accomplish in my life is to disentangle my identity from the identities of others. Most of us spend a disproportionate amount of our life's energies entangled in one another's personalities. We mistake other people's reactions to us, or comments about us, for what we actually are. I'm sitting in a bar and get a lecture from a slightly drunk truck driver sitting next to me that I'm an unshaven beatnik college student, and that I'm a coward because I'm against fighting the war in Vietnam. Immediately my hackles rise, and I feel attacked. I argue, defending myself as if he actually *did* have me pegged. What I should do is to simply remind myself that what he is describing is not me, but rather an image that he projects onto me due to his own inner mental-emotional state. *Then* I can argue with him if I want to.

I, like so many others in this culture, have been conditioned to ignore my own inner feelings, and to seek myself in the plethora of mirror images around me. Only by being aware of my own bodily and emotional states can I know my own stature—not from distorted mirrors that reflect either grandiose or diminutive images of me. To find out what is really around me, what is really me, on the one hand, and other people, on the other, I must, like the bull in the china shop, charge and smash through this sparkling array of mirrors. When the mirrors are all smashed to bits, I can see what they've been hiding.

At Stake Is a Chance for Survival

TIMOTHY C. EARLE*

OVER and against the confusion and fear which rule our lives, each of us attempts to press back upon the molding forces, to dent the form in his own way in order to avoid mortal structure and to create a dynamic order in which happy and creative existence is possible. Certain contemporary historical developments, however, indicate the coming into being of extremely powerful forces which act as limiting factors upon the possibilities of life style and individual growth. That is to say, for example, that there is a progressive possibility that a child born today anywhere in the world will grow up to become part of a Western-style industrialized society rather than of any of the other sorts of societies which have existed in the past. This imminent victory of science and technology over all of the world's populations will cause the proliferation among them of the diseases that we in the West have first experienced and have not as yet learned to control or even in a useful way to diagnose. The primary concerns of an intellectual leadership today, if it is to be a vital force in society, ought therefore to be the formation of knowledge about the destructive nature of social structures plus the development of theories of social change through which the great brutalizing forces of our era could be molded to fit human hands and minds, and thus be brought under control.

* *Timothy Earle, age twenty-five, began his college studies as a Mathematics major and is now a senior in the Department of Social Science, Interdisciplinary Studies. He plans to go on to graduate school in the social sciences and hopes to develop a career that will combine writing with some type of community work.*

This notion of the intellectual as social critic and as potential life-giver to society did not of course spontaneously form itself in my mind; it was impressed upon me by my experiences and finally given form by myself as a theory or set of ideas. Some bits of biography, history and criticism may serve to elucidate the genesis of my dissatisfaction and also the formulation of my theory.

The world into which I was born was in the throes of death. But of course to a small boy the war did not seem a grievous thing. It was a time when my hair could be slicked down over my eye and a comb pressed against my lip as I yelled "Heil Hitler!" and my friends sang that song about kicking Hitler in the pants. That's all it was to us: a kick in the pants and ration stamps and songs about Tojo. Oh, I had my victory garden in a wooden cheesebox which I placed upon the window sill; I did my part. But of course I didn't know anything about what was going on, that there was anything abnormal about the world as I found it. I noticed the change when good things like bubble gum came onto the market; but it wasn't until I got to school that the full portent of those events began to form in my mind.

A school is an institution established by a society for the purpose of educating children. Because of the inclusion of the ideal of universal education in the political ideology of America, it has become customary for the various states of the union to require children by law to attend an educational institution until they are approximately sixteen years old. This long, legally imposed period of indoctrination has proved itself to be one of the major reasons for the ever increasing strength of America as a nation. That is, the political power of the United States is due in part to the success of its educational system.

But it is not all that simple. The forming of people's lives, the bringing into being of new persons, is one of the most important functions and responsibilities of a society. Now, if education is such an important responsibility, *should* a society judge its educational system on the basis of its ability to produce citizens who, as educated persons, possess the qualities necessary to contribute to the further strengthening of the state?

Many Americans would be shocked at the notion of educating for the state—that's what they do behind the Iron Curtain or somewhere, not here in the U.S. But they would be mistaken. Though there are differences between the various political ideologies of the industrialized countries of the world, there exist in these countries only significant variations of one great educational ideology: to educate for the good of the country; that is, for the good of the nation-state. There is always a lot of talk about the "good of the child," but the fact is that whatever is truly good for the child is likely to be found, if at all, in a low position among a hierarchy of demands in an educational system. Among the primary demands are the demands of the state, and these demands are on the whole destructive of what is new and creative in a child. Education and creativity have always been contrary concepts. This should be obvious, but often those persons who claim to value creativity highly are the very same persons who romanticize about educational systems. But, then, these things are parts of the ideology.

Both the grammar school and high school which I attended were said to offer a good sort of education and, though their high reputations among the critics of the public schools may have been functions of the number of rich and influential persons whose children were involved, they probably were relatively successful in the fulfillment of their limited goals. Of course, the primary goal of all concerned, students, parents, administrators, teachers, janitors, coaches, counselors, everybody, was to secure for the students admission to the best possible colleges. Even though I came from a family the generations of which included no college graduates, I never contemplated any sort of activity after secondary school other than the continuation of the prepatterned educational process. My lower-class economic status did set limits upon my middle-class aspirations, however, by rendering me happily ignorant of the presumably important distinctions between the various universities in the area. I would go to the school to which I could go. In the same manner as the other schools I had attended, I wouldn't really choose between a number of possibilities. I would just go to whichever one it was possible for me to go to; it didn't really matter. Possessing no sort of leverage of my own with which to form the system to meet my needs, and having had what they call a typically limited lower-class urban field of experience, I had no choice other than to accept the role of student as defined by the system, thus fulfilling the needs of the system and not necessarily at the same time fulfilling my own.

Another consequence of the systematic tyranny of the school

business was that it was in the nature of things that, as I was an ignorant, unaware boy, I had to be told what I was and what I was to become. Thus it was determined as early as the grammar school years just what course of study I would follow. One aspect of the control which the state wields over the production of new citizens is seen clearly here. In my case I was informed that I possessed a scientific bent; I should take all of the mathematics and science courses which were offered and thus prepare myself for college and eventually for a well-paying job in industry. In short: industry (or government) needed scientists; I possessed the ability to become one and I was free of any commitment other than the vague desire to go to college. Therefore I would become a scientist in order to fulfill the expressed need. After all, it was they who were paying for all of the educational machinery.

The biases of the testing methods used are well known, but the awareness of a manipulative system does not manifest itself in a useful way to those being manipulated. A society gets what it wants from its productive systems: a particular system cannot be reformed without necessarily changing the structure of the society. And this is not allowed; power rules the day. The primary task of a culture is to preserve and perpetuate itself, and schools are the means through which these are accomplished. But the ignorant acceptance of a role by a person within a system, such as that of student, does not necessarily imply the eventual wrapping around oneself of the conditions of the role with a subsequent cessation of movement, growth and the stretching out for something new and alive. A person can also get smart; which is to say, a person can rebel.

We have thus arrived at one of the crucial problems of education in contemporary America. A school can be seen as an intermediary institution between the supposedly private life of the family and the public life of the society as a whole. The child, then, is first given the world as represented by the school; this is the law. The school must therefore accept the responsibility for presenting with authority a true representation of the world. But in contemporary America we are experiencing a progressive disintegration of authority due to a rejection on all sides of responsibility for the world, and this rejection of responsibility for the world is due in turn to the tragic and ever widening estrangement of men from the world.

My father was a perceptive man, artistically sensitive and a lover of life. Circumstances, however, prevented his ideas and fate from ever meeting in the creative hour. He had been a teacher for the WPA during the late thirties and early forties; but with the coming of World War II he took a job with the shipyards, and together with thousands of other men he labored to produce the machines which were to be used in the defeat of Fascism. After the war he was not able to recover his earlier status; he remained a laborer until he died, participating in none of the advertised benefits of being an American during a period of economic expansion. Such an experience of defeat, frustration and unfulfilled dreams creates a hatred in a man, a hopelessness which eats away a man's ties with society and eventually himself. While I was not taught to hate anything or anybody, and actually the contrary was true, I could not possibly be brought up in such an environment without becoming affected in such a way to make me aware of the tremendous destructive qualities of the American way of life.

There was, of course, a disparity between the world I knew actually existed for me and the world which was presented to me in high school by my teachers. This wasn't necessarily because the teachers did not know what was happening, though this might have been true. The basic causal factor was more likely to have been the rejection on the part of the teachers of any responsibility for what the world was. As was mentioned earlier, the consequence of such a rejection of responsibility is the subsequent disintegration of authority. The end product of this process is conflict in the mind of the student, confusion and ultimately an alienation from what seems to be a world of falsity and deceit. This alienation is balanced by an accompanying desperate grasping onto of whatever is the most immediate real bit of life. The absence of real adult authority therefore results in the individual student being placed at the mercy of the crowd. In the grip of a tyrannical majority a student is defenseless against pressures forcing him to do almost anything as payment for being allowed to feel real and vital and alive, even those things which may be most destructive to him as an individual.

Though I had tacitly accepted many of the middle-class goals which were presented to me in high school, I could not convince myself about the importance of certain processes on which the successful achievement of my goals was said to depend. An easy example is the grading system. It was absurd and that was it; hard as I tried, I couldn't believe in it. But then the whole system depended on it; it was supposed to have been somehow necessary. The unreality of that particular aspect of the system simply melted in with all of the other sorts of nebulous forms, presenting me with a holy mystery which I could not hope to comprehend. Any manipulation of the system to my own benefit was beyond possibility of being actualized. So I let myself be rolled along. Or I was rolled along, over the bumps and turns of the production line, to the end. I had faith that there would be something there, but I really didn't know or care.

While the consequences of an irresponsible society are often manifested in delinquent behavior, I was fortunate in that I had developed an early interest in athletics; it was in the playing of games that I came to create my most meaningful reality. I don't know if I can go so far as to say with Albert Camus that I learned all that I know of ethics through my participation in sports. But perhaps he was right. Vital participation is the basis of life; and it is difficult to conceive of any more likely place in America for the generation of ethical thought than on the hot asphalt of a big-city basketball court. A further fortunate aspect of this for me was that I was not overly proficient in any particular game; I was just good enough to play. Thus the group from which I derived my identity in high school was the group with which I played games; it was the best of all possible groups. It was an egalitarian brotherhood in which there was no real dominance; the good players who were heroes to those who didn't know them, were simply members of the group. And money or good looks and clothes had no effect on what happened when a boy was in uniform playing a game. I enjoyed that very much; it was a happy time then.

Estrangement or alienation, as a basis for the rejection of responsibility, the loss of authority and the proliferation of immoral behavior, is thus seen to be one of the most important manifestations of the diseases of modern industrial society, especially in America. Thus far I have sketched in a brief way a few of the meanings which I had developed in the world of my high-school years. Between then and now, from boy to man, many things happened. For the purposes of this essay I shall partition those years into three distinct periods, though in actuality they were not at all disjoint, but overlapping and mixed. The periods are: the work period, the army period and the college period; each of these could be subtitled, respectively: resistance, war and rebellion.

I had joined the Teamster's Union when I was sixteen; it was the same local to which my father belonged, and with his help I was able to get work. It was a wonderful experience; I was a fellow worker among real men. They used their bodies to make good wages; and they used their minds to outsmart the bosses. The guy who came around to the warehouse to collect the union dues wore a sport coat with wide, brightly colored stripes and padded shoulders; his shirt was a dark color and his tie was red. He smoked a cigar and had a checkered felt hat on his head with a large yellow feather stuck in the band. He smelled like he had just gotten back from the track, and maybe he needed some money.

In high school I was always the champion of labor and liberalism. I was in love with trade-unionism, F.D.R., Truman and Stevenson. The whole American liberal democratic tradition was my special province, and I had faith in it; despite the many conflicting notions I had of the world, I clung to the liberal faith. But knowledge sometimes has a curing power, the power to cure oneself of the distortions of a fading ideology.

Early in his short history, man used tools to shape his world; he was the master and controller of the world he made. But then labor replaced work, and the free use of tools by men developed into a unification of the implement with the body; the motion and rhythm of the laboring process came to determine the motion and rhythm of life. Ever since the industrial revolution man has lived in a world of machines, and these machines have controlled and eventually replaced his labor. Electricity was controlled and made useful, and recently the culminating phase of automation has been reached. In the automatic mode of production, the process is self-controlled, and just as in the laboring process where the distinction between man and machine became unclear, in automation the distinction between machine and product is blurred. The automation or cybernation revolution, then, has replaced human nervous systems just as surely as the industrial revolution replaced human muscle. The problem, as expressed by Hannah Arendt, is "whether machines still serve the world and its things, or if, on the contrary, they and the automatic motion of their processes have begun to rule and even destroy the world and things."[1]

As Marx continually pointed out, the world of machines is not the "real" world, it is a substitute world, an alien world. During the industrial revolution man's labor was alienated, but in the cybernation revolution there is more to be lost, more than Marx could foretell. Automated machines have become less and less like things of the world, the products of man; they are becoming more and more like living organisms. This hyper-alienation of man, this emptying out of himself, body and brain, into his environment during the cybernation revolution is proceeding at an ever increasing rate. Donald Michael was obviously concerned where he wrote: ". . . the frustration and pointlessness [produced] may well evoke, in turn, a war of desperation—ostensibly against some external enemy but, in fact, a war to make the world safe for human beings by destroying most of society's sophisticated technological base. One thing is clear: if the new 'logic' is to resolve the problems raised here, it will have to generate beliefs, behavior, and goals far different from those which we have held until now and which are driving us more and more inexorably into a contradictory world run by (and for?) ever more intelligent, ever more versatile slaves."[2] The misery of man is increasing, but it is not, as Marx predicted, a material misery. It is an infinitely more dangerous and destructive misery, a misery of the soul; and it could be the terminal misery of man.

After I was graduated from high school, I experienced for a time that malady which afflicts so many millions of persons in America, the inability to find an honest job. So, I took a dishonest one; I became a salesman. Thus the generations progress, improving one over the other toward the Great Society; I had my white collar while my father died with a blue one around his neck. The firm for which I

[1] Hannah Arendt, *The Human Condition,* Garden City, New York, Doubleday Anchor Books, 1959, p. 132.

[2] Donald N. Michael, *Cybernation: The Silent Conquest,* Santa Barbara, California, The Center for the Study of Democratic Institutions, 1962, p. 46.

worked was a member of a nationwide chain of department stores, a factory for the production of controlled acquisitive satisfaction among a series of such factories. I came to hate it there and was finally fired for not giving a damn. America, to many people all over the world, is personified in the form of the Great Salesman, and her philosophy is best known as Salesmanship. These symbols do not of course reveal the true depth and value of America; but they have for so long enveloped her people, oozed into their pores and fogged their minds that it is difficult to hope that these detested things will ever be overcome.

I can't say that the three years I spent as a member of the U.S. Army were entirely wasted. Actually I had a hell of a good time during most of the tour. I saw the world and learned a bit about it, and I enjoyed immensely the fellowship which was the result of the generation by the officers of a common consciousness among the enlisted men. Indeed, we all did have a common enemy; but only a few of us took it really seriously. To take an enemy seriously means, I think, to treat him as a man and also to attempt an understanding of what has caused the confrontation. That is, I could not hate an officer because he was an officer; nor could I, as they say, respect his rank. It was not the men who ruled my life who were my enemy, it was the system. Abstract as it may see, it was real for me and for many others who were with me. And when it is a whole system you must fight, you must use sabotage, which is to say that you must limit your cooperation with it to that minimum level which is at once most effective and consistent with your own well-being. It was an art, really; and it was in that conflict that I created my meanings during those years. Odd, isn't it, that a man should be forced to derive meaningful life in a petty conflict with the most horrendously powerful system of destruction ever put together by the hands of men? Odd and absurd and tragic, I think.

If one were asked to choose a date which, in the twentieth century, symbolized the historical evolution from the epoch of the Industrial Revolution to the epoch of the Scientific Revolution, one possible answer would be 1945. In that year man took it upon himself to liberate on earth the powers of the universe. It is hardly possible to exaggerate the significance of that event; man had become absolute, and because he was absolute, with the cosmic power to destroy himself, he had become all but totally alienated from his real self. C. Wright Mills bluntly summarized the situation this way: "The position amounts to this: We are at the very end of the military road. It leads nowhere but to death. With war, all nations will fall. Yet the preparation of World War III is the most strenuous and massive effort of the leading societies of the world today. War has become total. And war has become absurd."[3]

How has this come about? Hasn't war throughout much of human history been a gallant, heroic, even religious thing? If we are at the end of the military road, how did we get there? A brief sketch, following Gunther Anders' analysis, provides some answers to these questions. First of all there is the reality of a singular death. When one man kills another man, there is a parity of cause and effect; it is possible for the producer to react to his product. The phenomenon of war has evolved from its early beginnings in man-to-man combat through various stages of technological development. These refinements have progressively increased the disparity between cause and effect, until finally it is now totally impossible to comprehend the effects of the War Game. Man as a producer has been split apart from man as a being with human reactions; there is no guilt, nor is there fear. Total power has produced total helplessness. Anders draws this conclusion: "In fact, the helplessness with which contemporary mankind reacts—or rather fails to react—to the existence of the superbomb bespeaks a lack of freedom the like of which has never before existed in history. . . . Truly unfree, divested of all dignity, definitively the most deprived of men are those confronted with situations and things with which they cannot cope by definition, to which they are unequal linguistically, intellectually, and emotionally—ourselves."[4] This all-but-total alienation, this schizoid personality of modern man, is the prime fact of contemporary life.

My job in the Army was to gather intelligence, the military euphemism for spying. It was interesting because, even at the low-echelon level at which I operated, I could learn to appreciate the

[3] C. Wright Mills, *The Causes of World War III,* New York, Simon and Schuster, 1958, pp. 18–19.

[4] Gunther Anders, "Reflections on the H Bomb," *Dissent,* Spring, 1956.

workings of military logic and the absurdly incredulous behavior which is the product of such thinking. My period of enlistment spanned the various Cuban and Berlin crises; I was thus able to observe from the inside a bit of the monster whose shadow, in recent years, has lengthened so as to threaten the entire world with an eternal darkness.

Slowly, during those years I came to change; or, to put it another way, I became more aware of what I really was and what was happening all around me. I had learned that the liberal faith, the faith which had sustained me as a boy and in which I had placed my hope for a better life, this faith had become banal and its force was no longer cooperative with the vital forces of life; rather, it had become one of the greatest destructive forces in human history. It was in interaction with this force that I first came to accept what amounted to a crude sort of pacifist political posture. So formless was it in fact that I didn't really think of myself as being a pacifist until I was labeled as such in the newspaper coverage of a demonstration in which I participated shortly after my separation from the army. Since that time I have been engaged mainly in the educational process; this has enabled me to elaborate and to clarify some of my ideas and also to examine the relationship between the educational establishment, or what ought to be the saving force in society, and the society it ought to save.

There exists in America a systematic attempt on the part of the established educational elite to move the line of demarcation between the world of the adult and the world of the child to a progressively older age. This attempt is one aspect of the general trend in America toward a lifelong childhood, a wonderful, carefree existence in which one is never anguished by responsibility to the real world of adult human beings. The general trend in turn is due to the reluctance on the part of those with power to allow the creative and revolutionary things brought into the world by new people to ever be actualized by adults. Power must be defended against what is new. But if there are no responsible adults to manifest what is new in useful ways, then what is created is simply diffused into the mass of society, thus precluding it from having any effect toward substantive change.

Against this trend toward a society of children, there exists, it seems to me, a contrary force, the tendency toward political activity, i.e., responsible adult activity on the part of the younger members of society. The struggle between these two conflicting forces has come to be centered at the college years, and it is now being fought on campuses all over America. The importance of this struggle, simplified here, would be difficult to overestimate; at stake is a chance for survival.

How did this felicitous contrary force, this force for life, come into being? And what were the social sources of its formation? During the past year, there have been any number of analyses presented on this matter; but none of them, I believe, has revealed the roots of the problem. It's not that the roots are buried so deeply, though it is instructive to observe that the depth of the probe is generally determined in inverse proportion to the depth to which the commentator's feet are sunk into established soil. It is just that there are so many of them that one must choose which roots one wishes to use, which ones he will call the factual roots. And just as the depth of the probe is determined by one's position in relation to the Establishment, so too one's view of the roots is determined by one's position in relation to the tree. My view, of course, is from somewhere within the tree, perhaps the end of a limb, but hopefully toward its heart.

I choose in my analysis to use alienation theory, and I do so simply because it seems to me the best available tool toward the revelation of what I consider valuable information. In other words, my methodology is determined in part by the results I wish to acquire. Now, the high-powered liberal commentators are very put off by the alienation theories. Lewis Feuer,[5] for example, has denounced alienation as being perhaps true, but nevertheless useless; he chose instead to present a psychoanalytical-generational conflict theory. I would call that theory irrelevant and useless. Further, I would claim that Feuer for some reason or other, perhaps because of his ex-radical background, chose to misinterpret the meaning of alienation. In the following sketch I will attempt to present a possible example, patterned after the model developed by Marvin B. Scott,[6] of how alienation theory can be applied to college students.

[5] Lewis Feuer, "Rebellion at Berkeley," *The New Leader,* December 21, 1964.

[6] Marvin B. Scott, "The Social Sources of Alienation," in Irving Louis Horowitz, ed., *The New Sociology,* New York, Oxford University Press, 1965.

Scott first of all presents the elements which necessarily constitute socially meaningful behavior. They are: (1) values; (2) norms; (3) organization of roles; and (4) situational facilities. Using this basic structure, Scott concludes that "from a sociological point of view . . . the sources of alienation are to be found in the lack of a) commitment to values; b) conformity to norms; c) responsibility; and d) control of facilities. Consistent with this perspective, one may speak of alienation from values, norms, roles, and facilities." I will deal with these points in reverse order, from the bottom to the top of the hierarchy.

First of all, the college student is alienated from his facilities. Now, a student's facilities are the means by which he can perform his role. The question, then, is whether, given an acceptance of his role by the student, the means at his disposal are sufficient for his proper performance of his role. The means in question constitute the entire structure of the university system. For example, the professors: Are there enough of them? Are they disposed toward the fulfilling of their responsibilities as teachers? Are they teaching what the students feel they ought to be taught? Have they been responsible persons in relation to the world, and thereby won the respect of the students and the right to authority? There is only one answer to all of these questions and many others similar to them, and that is No. Teachers were called by C. Wright Mills the "economic proletarians of the professions" and, since the idea of the proletariat is anathema to the American mind, the teaching profession has not attracted its share of the most talented people. In recent years, however, sources of income for properly placed college professors have made those positions progressively more attractive. By "properly placed" I mean professors in the various sciences who can produce some marketable product through the workings of their research apparatus. In this way many men have rallied staffs of graduate assistants around their projects and, in the course of producing new military tactics or, perhaps, quicker methods of consumer duping, have managed to live very comfortably indeed. Therefore the current sorts of economic inducements offered to the professors tend not to lessen the problem of student-teacher relations but rather to make it all the more acute and alienating. Added to this are all of the related problems of departmentalism, vested interests in certain intellectual points of view, and the gamut of irresponsible and cowardly actions in the face of the slightest threat from the real world out there. These are all legitimate grievances which the student has against just one aspect of the university structure. When the list is expanded to include such things as financing, housing, classrooms, buildings, libraries, books, etc., it takes on the form of a full-scale critique of educational structures, and there is no room for that here. In summary, I can say that the means, as given, do not support, and are in part even destructive of the proper performance of the student's role and, most importantly, are not at all under his control. The student is therefore alienated from the facilities which he must use in order to perform his role.

The second aspect of alienation on our college campuses is the alienation of the student from his role as "student." The role "student" is of course created by the society in which the student exists. Thus a student is responsible in his role if he fulfills the expectations which society has created for that role. If he does not fulfill the expectations of society, then he is not responsible and is alienated from his role. It is certainly clear that society, in this case the Great American Taxpayer (henceforth referred to as G.A.T.) and all of his friends and advisors, holds a radically differing interpretation of the role "student" from that which is held by those persons who are involved in being educated. For example, there is the perennial problem of the relationship between politics and education. The G.A.T. tends in all his cultural innocence to claim a classic separation between the two. All the while, of course, he insists on a thorough political indoctrination for the little ones who pass through the citizen factories which he has had assembled with his grudgingly given greenbacks. It is the most obvious of his hypocrisies. American education has always been political in the belief that democracy depended upon a well-indoctrinated citizenry; much of its content has been propaganda for the glories of democracy and the free enterprise system. This in itself is not bad; it is inevitable, really, but it should at least be recognized. Moreover, the recent trend has been toward an ever increasing dominance of the economic aspects of this propaganda over the political. That is, in direct proportion to the decline of liberalism as a workable political ideology and its consequent hardening into a destructive moral theology, the G.A.T. has forced a shift in educational emphasis from the distracting doctrines of democracy to the cancerous concepts of capitalism.

But what about the student? Does he see himself as a mini-monopolist or an immature imperialist? Does he feel that all he needs is a little bit of learning and that then he too can grow up to be a G.A.T., that he too can control and exploit just about whatever he feels? Is this what he wants? Of course the answer is No. What the G.A.T. does not realize is that young people today are far more liberated persons than was the case in the past. This means that if political and economic propaganda are inevitable defense mechanisms used by the old folks as protection against the young, then they should be terminated at an early stage, phased out at least by the end of secondary school. No, I don't suspect that this will happen, but it would help; it would be smart and it would ameliorate the crisis. Today's student sees himself as someone who is really studying. He believes that what he studies for should be his own business, the product of his own person interacting with his own environment. Not the G.A.T.'s. My point here is that there exists a tremendous disparity between the role "student" as created by the American Establishment and what in fact the American student of today wants and needs to be. Thus the student is alienated from his role and feels no responsibility for fulfilling it.

The third aspect of alienation is a lack of conformity to norms, the norms being the proper means of obtaining a stated goal or value. This, I believe, is the most crucial issue involved in the alienation theory. While it is true that the selection of the value in the first place seems to be somewhat arbitrary and dependent upon all those factors that form one's philosophical outlook, it is in dealing with the means that one comes into conflict with other persons who may share one's value but who do not happen to believe that one's means are "proper." But there is, it seems to me, an organic connection between the value and the means such that, whatever the particular value to which one is committed, it cannot be approached save by the means that are proper to it. This of course is true regardless of the means deemed proper by the powers in society. Conversely, the means determine the value. There are, therefore, no absolute values, since the means are not absolute but only what is thought to be meaningful behavior on the part of an historical man. Nothing is certain of realization. Albert Camus put it this way: "Does the end justify the means? That is possible. But what will justify the end? To that question, which historical thought leaves pending, rebellion replies: the means."[7] This sort of moral approach to the sociology of knowledge is one of the peculiar aspects of the new student generation and it is, I believe, the most significant manifestation of their alienation from the liberal educational establishment.

The possible consequences of the students' alienation from norms will include a radical calling to task by the students of those professors who still claim to preach the truth. Difficult questions will be asked; there will be conflict, and the battleground will be epistemology. All claims to expertise will be examined, and those professors found guilty of sham and hypocrisy will be called fools and gently ignored. When the students are through, there will be only men, students and scholars, each committed to his own values, socially formed but individually organized and free. With a common consciousness they will tell all those who wish to buy death from the university community to go to hell. Then they will go to the seats of government, merchants of destruction no more, and they will tell those experts who run and ruin their lives that they all are fools and that they aren't running anything or anybody anymore. The people are going to make it themselves, they will tell them; join us and see what it's like. And the intellectual community will spread the word from America that the experts are all gone and that men are really free. They will hear the good news in Russia, in Germany and France. In England they'll hear it and in Italy and Spain. Europe will be free, and then Latin America and Canada and Africa and China. The world will be free. A man will say to another man that he could not live unless the other also lived; that the very fact and quality of his own existence depended upon his dialogue with the other. If I kill you, he will say, I will also in the same blow kill myself. But, I want to live; I am life. How can I die and still be me? So we will both live, and we will build a community where there is no manipulative

[7] Albert Camus, *The Rebel,* New York, Vintage Books, 1956, p. 292.

government and there are no experts. Each man will be dependent upon the others for his life; yet each man will be individually free. And that's the most convincing story I can remember ever having heard. It's about how the student rebellion saved the world.

Live and Let Live

CONNELL PERSICO*

FOR some time students have been working in slums, marching in demonstrations, sitting-in, burning draft cards and going on hunger strikes. A great deal has been written about them. Their actions have contributed to the passing of considerable legislation. And they have been called a great many names. If the pursuit of a vision born in this country almost two hundred years ago is to continue, it is necessary to take a look at these young people who have been so active in the 1960s and to develop an understanding among all generations of Americans.

Some say this student awakening began as a movement with the first lunch counter sit-in in the South in early 1960. Others date it from the City Hall anti-HUAC[1] demonstration in San Francisco in May of 1960. Some even believe it started as a reaction against the so-called silent generation. How strange today sounds the statement written in 1959 by Clark Kerr, President of the University of California: "The employers will love this generation; they are not going to press many grievances. . . . They are going to be easy to handle. There aren't going to be any riots."[2] This able scholar was apparently looking at the fifties just ending, rather than at the new decade about to take shape. Like so many other experts, he was wrong.

* *Connell Persico, age twenty-two, is a senior in Political Science. He has been active in student government and civil rights. He plans to become a writer and college professor.*

1 House Un-American Activities Committee of the United States Congress.

2 Quoted in Jack Newfield, "Revolt Without Dogma," *Motive*, Vol. XXVI, No. 1, October, 1965, p. 21.

When 1960 rolled around, the quiet was broken by a thundering wave of young people trying to find themselves in their society.

Much confusion reigned over this new activity. Some people felt it necessary to find names for us. And, of course, the usual ones came first: rebels, radicals, subversives and Communists. The names soon became more refined and positive: New Moralists, New Anarchists, the Committed Generation, and so on. We don't want those names under which we've been grouped. They imply that there is something strange about us, different from other people. They create a chasm between us and other people. And it's not true that all of us distrust everyone over thirty! Why can't you see us for what we are? We are your own sons and daughters, not someone far away to be read about in a newspaper.

Human beings are what we are—flesh, blood, conscience, emotions, intellect. Like everybody else, we, too, worry about the mystery known as life. We're unfulfilled lovers trying to introduce compassion as the means and ends of international relations. We're amateur artists painting a landscape of blending whites, reds, browns, blacks and yellows. We're stumbling poets creating an ode to the beauty of all men everywhere. We're simply human beings trying to maintain our integrity.

So we have been marching, sitting-in, getting arrested, and going to jail over free speech, civil rights, and Vietnam. The FBI attributes our actions to Communist influence. Others attempt to find some other external force that is supposed to be pressuring us into direct action. Each time a demonstration takes place, people look past the demonstrators for an explanation. They ought to look into the eyes of the people who are marching. They would find that every pair of eyes tells a different story. Every one of the thousands who has become involved in this revolution has his own particular motives and reasons. There are Stalinists, Trotskyites and Maoists; there are Republicans and Democrats; there are opportunists and know-nothings; there are people who can't tell you why they are participating—they just feel that they have to do *something*. There are the nonviolent people and the egg-throwers; there are people with nothing but questions; and others with all the answers. Yet for all of our differences, we come together and pursue a common interest. We feel compelled to work for a life that is worth living.

How I wish I could explain the joy, the beauty, the warmth that emanate from the camaraderie we have. It's not the blind discipline of any dogma or ideology that brings us together. We're all searching for answers to the same age-old questions: Who am I? Why am I here? As people of the mid-twentieth century, we feel that cooperation among humans is the only road to survival. We've wrapped up our freedom with the freedom of all men; our personal peace with the peace of the world. We enjoy being together because the spirit unleashed frees us to be fully human. We come together, live together, rarely condemning, always trying to understand, and always attempting to relate to each other and the world with compassion and respect. The ideals that bring us together are peace, equality, freedom and justice. These are also the concrete realities that we work for. They are our common bond. It's not our victories nor the publicity we gain that give us our strength and keep us together. It's our sense of community, our being human. For we have seen how difficult it is to live a full life alone. We separate sadly, for alone we stumble and fall, and our vision becomes hazy.

We've all of us in one way or another been afraid: afraid to come of age in the America of the sixties; afraid of its complacency and apathy; afraid of its affluence. We had thought life would be the way we were taught it would be, and yet we saw something different in the way adult Americans actually live. So we set out to create a better world based on our country's traditions and heritage, a world we had thought already existed. We were not going to let the "affluent society" dictate how we should act, so we developed our own concepts of morality and integrity. We've found a way of living that we feel presents more hope for mankind as a whole and individually. Our motto could be "Live and let live," for among us no one tells anyone else how to live, or how to be accepted, or how to become a success; everyone is left on their own, to develop their own ideas of life and love.

As for myself, I was afraid even of my peers and their lives, for I couldn't kick some of the morality I'd learned that kept me from living the way they did. For a while, I existed in both worlds, the world of the "middle class" and the world of the "new breed." I felt I couldn't be comfortable living totally in either. But after a long struggle with my fears, after facing up to myself, I am coming to understand that I have no one else to answer to for my life, that I can live as I want to, as a unique individual. And there are thousands of us, rebuking affluence and so-called middle-class values. We're trying out a whole range of values and ideas in order to find our own ways of being individuals in this modern American society. This may involve seeking acceptance, for who wants to be alone, to have no one to share dreams, feelings and thoughts with? It may even involve hating you and all we see you as standing for. But most of all, it's a grand experiment in living as total human beings. And isn't it only natural to identify this individual struggle for freedom with all who are oppressed everywhere? Doesn't that help to create a base of understanding among us? And doesn't it show that all of us, no matter what age or outlook, are really allies and friends?

So next time we are marching for civil rights or to protest the Vietnam war, don't condemn us as unpatriotic or subversive. Understand that we are people like you trying to create a better world for all, people trying to figure out what's happening in the world, what its possibilities are, and how we can honestly relate to them. We don't ask that you accept our tactics. (Many of us wish there were other ways.) We don't even ask that you approve of us as people. All we ask is that you try to understand why we are there, why we are concerned, why we are giving up the guaranteed material security of a college degree for the sake of problems that seemingly are not even ours. Why do we worry about freedom, equality, and peace, when we could be so comfortable if we would only forget about them? Why are we willing to experience mental and physical pain over a woman burned by napalm in a Vietnamese village, when we could be soaking up sun on a beach?

I was born eighteen months before the destruction of Hiroshima and Nagasaki. I grew up in the Eisenhower era. The most vivid experience of my early life was McCarthyism. My mother apparently couldn't get it into her head that at the time you either had to give up your beliefs or remain silent. So she went on writing and talking about the injustices she saw. And she took me to meetings where people were talking about the Rosenbergs and Alger Hiss. I remember her being branded a Communist because she was teaching the

Declaration of Independence and the Bill of Rights, along with how important it is to stick to your beliefs. At one point I remember being sent off to another school because someone had written in my brother's religion book, "Your mother is a Red." Most of the time I played baseball and rode my bike—that other stuff was for grownups. But I listened and learned. Then, after a while, I started reading on my own—the Hardy Boys series, Thomas Paine, Jefferson, Thoreau, and other Americana. And by 1956 I knew enough about American politics to understand why my first hero, Adlai Stevenson, lost the presidential election.

These early educational experiences were supplemented by the fact that I've attended a total of thirteen different schools. This not only helped me to develop means of survival without a group of friends but also tended to build up a strong sense of insecurity. As a result, though I learned to do things on my own—mainly reading about American politics, culture and social problems—I grew up lacking, yet always desiring the warmth and fun of true friends. Many other events have gone into making me what I am—accidents, prolonged illnesses, deaths in my family, people I've met, and probably a lot of things I don't even remember.

My thirteenth school was San Francisco State College. It was there that I began developing my own view of the world. This college first provided me with the freedom, encouragement and intellectual tools to begin finding myself and my place in this society that seemed too big and frightening. When I entered State in 1961, we had just been through an anti-HUAC demonstration and the trials that followed and needed to talk about the whys and wherefores of our actions, what had happened, and where we were going from there. We wanted to talk about how we were and what we could do in this world. So we set up a makeshift platform and began speaking about civil rights. We collected money and distributed literature. And it all happened without a Free Speech Movement, thanks to an alert and progressive administration. No college official ever told us to be quiet. Instead, they sat down, drew up and got approval for a statement of philosophy that recognized students as adults and guaranteed for them all the rights and responsibilities of full citizens.

Is this any way to run a college? You bet it is! People can become educated only if they can ask those "controversial" questions that shake the base of our system, those questions that are necessary to understand the paradoxes of our society. How can people find out what they can do about injustice, if they can't get together with other people who feel the same way?

With no battle to wage against a college administration denying our rights, we could concentrate on the important issues of peace, freedom and equality. We marched through San Francisco in protest against the Birmingham bombings, we sat-in at the Sheraton Palace Hotel on behalf of nondiscriminatory employment, we got arrested on Automobile Row for the same struggle, and we supported our brethren over at Berkeley when they began insisting on the same freedom we had already had for three years. Through it all, San Francisco State College provided a forum where we could not only decide what to do in each situation that came up, but also discuss the results. The pros and cons of any action would be discussed freely and openly and each person would be made aware not only of his responsibilities but also of the possible consequences of his behavior. Ah, what beautiful agony we often went through as we struggled with the question of personal participation and all the moral and practical considerations it seemed to involve!

Then in March, 1965, a group of us became so disturbed by the events in Selma, Alabama, that we decided to leave school for a couple of weeks and travel there to do what we could. I'll never forget walking round the campus the Sunday before we left. An eighteen-year-old friend and I struggled with the whys of the situation, eyes filled with tears, hearts filled with fear, minds filled with doubt. He couldn't understand why he had to become a man at eighteen, why there weren't enough adults fighting against injustice so that he could stay home, why it was his responsibility to bring about civil rights for others. We never did resolve these dilemmas, but as we left we received a note from a friend: "We sometimes must do what we have to do, rather than what we want to do."

We arrived in Selma a few days later—tired, hungry, scared, wanting to do something, anything. We marched; we sang; we went to jail; we listened; and we learned. The evening before we went out marching, we practiced how to fall. When it came time to march into the aroused white community's home ground, six of us stood in the street asking one another, "Is it worth it?" "Do you think we'll be beaten or killed?" "Can you stand the pain?" And then we marched. When the verse of "We Shall Overcome" which begins "We are not afraid" came around, we sang loud enough for the whole United States to hear us. For the fact was that we were afraid. But we knew that by concerted action, by many acting as one, we *would* overcome.

We were Americans at last; we weren't really afraid—shaking and defecating in our pants, yes, but afraid, no; we were in the field, working for the ideals that were all we knew as great in America: equality, justice, freedom. And we were side by side with other Americans: all those beautiful black people who had faced fear and through it had become strong. They imbued us with a new patriotism, a new vision of the American dream. And they made me recognize my prejudices; I came face to face with my feelings for the Negro, and they weren't ideal. But one field worker said, "Me too, baby, I don't like you white men either, but we can work it out." And so we marched together and bridged the gap that misunderstanding and separation had created. For it had been fear that we had feared, and once having overcome that fear, we marched almost serenely, even knowing that we might be killed. As other men had faced death on various foreign battlefields for what they believed America represented, so we were willing to die right here at home. Heroic? No. Martyrs? No. Just young people trying to relate themselves to their society, trying to create a world with which they could in good conscience identify. When we left Selma we knew the world hadn't changed very much, if at all, but each of us had a new understanding of the Southern dilemma, and each of us had a new vision of brotherhood, community, and America's potential. All of us came back a little more human, a little less afraid to live as we are.

If it hadn't been for the free, inquiring kind of education I enjoyed at San Francisco State College, I probably wouldn't have been there. If I hadn't had the opportunity to open my mind and to develop a feeling for the world as adults and humans, I could not have ever understood the great meanings of Selma. I had that opportunity because my alma mater offers those who attend it a chance to participate in the educational process as policy-makers and educators. It acknowledges the right of students to a full voice in the kind of education they are to receive. The results are exciting. Thanks to the efforts of the last four student governments, and a gentle nudge by the F.S.M., students now participate in every decision affecting the campus. They have a seat and vote on all faculty and administrative boards and committees. They have initiated a new, student-organized program in General Education, with its own specially designed courses and hand-picked professors. Working together with members of the faculty and administration, they have established an "experimental college"—an informal, educational focus within the college as a whole and intended to explore politically and humanly relevant topics that the regular curriculum passes over, among them the topic of "Nonviolence in a Violent World." And the whole operation has been student-led the whole way. It has been possible only because of the mutual trust among all campus elements—students, faculty and administration alike. As a result, there's been no energy wasted on internal feuds. Instead, there's a concerted effort on the part of all concerned to make the education offered at the College the very best in the country. And if present trends continue, it will be education for the full development of total human beings—people who will be informed, capable of thinking and creating, and sensitive to the issues of our times.

Isn't that what education should be? Why study only how things have been, or how they are right now? Isn't that only background preparation? Isn't the most urgent question of all the challenge of how to develop a world in which one can live peacefully, ethically, honestly, and in a way to help people work out their individual and collective problems? Isn't that what the curriculum should be most concerned about? If this concern for humanity and personal growth is the real business of education, the present grading system is a hindrance and an anachronism. If education is to be a humanizing process, an occasion to help young people to find themselves and develop their own unique relationship to their society, how can such an experience be graded? What can a grade of average, above average, or excellent mean? There is no need for competitiveness in education conceived in this manner. It can do no good, only a lot of harm. There is need only for freedom of exploration and understanding, and for respect and personal encouragement. The object must be to help each person to confront himself, to find his own meanings and purposes, and to overcome his fears of living, loving, and being himself. For while there is always someone to tell us what is good and bad for us and how we ought to live, only the individual can know what is really best for himself. Education should provide the means for each person to find this out. Its job isn't done by merely offering courses of study in specific fields. These are important. But the student is only secondarily a student. He is first and last a human being. And his education has to be attuned to him as such.

Contemporary formal education makes one serious mistake. Too great a portion of the energies of colleges and universities is still devoted to the expansion of the intellect, at the expense of the emotions. Since education should be the means of developing the total person, much greater emphasis should be devoted to the exploration and understanding of emotions. Everywhere I look I see people of all age levels and groups being afraid of their feelings, of love, of their common humanity. I know how afraid of these dimensions of my life I have been myself; it finally took help through counseling to break down those fears. For I am looking for people, a community, and I rarely find them through discussions of political science or any other exclusively analytical discipline. I find them through struggling with people about the questions of love, what it means to be alive, and what life's purposes can and ought to be.

It is not only for our individual sakes that we must overcome the fear of our emotions. It is also for our life as a society. For when we are captives of fear, we become manipulatable by anyone who understands how to trigger and direct our fears. In this way fear weakens our ability to be ethical people. It was this, I think, that Franklin D. Roosevelt was getting at in his speech of March 4, 1933, when he said, "So first of all, let me assert my firm belief that the only thing we have to fear is fear itself—nameless, unjustified terror which paralyzes needed efforts to convert retreat into advance."[3] These words, it seems to me, get to the heart of the problem of all mankind. They apply not only to our lives and relations as individuals but to human dealings within and among nations. The evidence is all around

[3] Ben D. Zevin, ed., *Nothing to Fear,* New York, Popular Library, 1961, p. 26.

us that people are afraid. They are afraid to become involved with anyone or anything that may affect their material security. They are afraid to risk their paycheck to speak out against discrimination or government policy. They are afraid to risk being rejected or ridiculed for questioning generally accepted beliefs. No, I don't condemn them. But I do say that people are afraid and that it undermines their moral capabilities and that the time comes when we have to overcome these fears and take our stand. It's a great feeling to be able to stand in front of one's mirror and look oneself in the eyes! But first one has to recognize that one has been afraid.

The same thing applies to our government, with its priceless heritage. It pays lip service to America's high ideals, and then does the opposite. It also seems afraid of being its real self. Engaged in a war that everyone knows is a mistake, our government refuses to withdraw or negotiate with the "enemy" for fear of loss of face. It too is afraid. And it would rather risk destruction than admit its mistake. How ignoble, how unmanly, how fearful! Our government is afraid of America and would rather shatter the mirror than look in it. And yet how else to become strong and healthy again except to confront its fears?

But our country has so many riches and gadgets and busy-nesses that keep it from facing up to its real feelings, needs and opportunities. I was for a long time distracted by these things myself. As far as material things go, America has provided me with a comfortable existence. Rarely have I gone without food, clothing, or other necessities. In fact, I've rarely gone without a good many luxuries. I've traveled throughout the United States and was able to spend one summer in Europe. I've had a good education at minimal cost, and after graduation I'll have the potential to earn more money than is necessary to exist. I have the world by the tail because I am an American, and yet I'm not content, for all around me I see people denied what I have and can have. I've worked in a tutorial program in one of San Francisco's "poverty pockets" and have seen the vicious circle that prohibits the people living there from escaping. I'm powerless to do anything about it, and yet I know this country has the resources and the ability to help these people help themselves. What keeps our government from taking rapid, radical steps to alleviate these problems? The War on Poverty has so far proved mainly a farce and has effected little change. There have to be jobs, education and re-education, an eradication of slums, and a direct encounter with discrimination. Our government makes halfhearted stabs at these problems but fails to meet them head on. Why? Is it late middle age that keeps our country from experimenting? The willingness to see ever new challenges in life has been the source of our unique strength. Have we now grown altogether afraid of risks? Are we on the decline, a stagnant society content to revel in its past glories and eventually to die with nothing but a whimper? Or can we become visionaries again, casting away our fears and plunging headlong, with national pride and integrity, into the battle for equality at home and a fuller life for all men everywhere?

America has not only provided me with the material necessities and an education for which I am thankful. She has also bred me on the finest ideals any nation ever espoused. Take the Declaration of Independence: "We hold these truths to be self-evident, that all men are created equal, that they are endowed by their Creator with certain unalienable Rights, that among these are Life, Liberty and the pursuit of Happiness." Take our Bill of Rights, with which we are all familiar. Take Woodrow Wilson's moving statement in *The New Freedom:* "How always have men's hearts beat as they saw the coast of America rise to their view! How it has always seemed to them that the dweller there would be rid of kings, of privileged classes, and of all those bonds which had kept men depressed and helpless, and would there realize the full fruition of his sense of honest manhood, would there be one of a great body of brothers, not seeking to defraud and deceive one another, but seeking to accomplish the general good."[4] This is what America has always meant to me. Weren't you too once caught up with a dream that America was the land of equality, and opportunity, an enormous community where each person would help his neighbor, where all would work together for the common good? And yet look around us.

In the midst of our riches, there are millions who remain poor, ignorant and neglected. And all our government's much-publicized

[4] Finley Foster and Homer Watt, eds., *Voices of Liberty,* New York, Macmillan, 1941, p. 207.

efforts to help them are in effect mere political gestures insufficient even to keep up with the rate of human deterioration involved. The rest of us are wallowing in consumer goods, most of which by now we could live without, and to pay for which we remain ever in debt and harnessed to jobs that mean little to us but money. So absorbed in this high-priced prosperity have we become that we have lost our capacity for human adventure. As our late President, John F. Kennedy, said, "It is a harsh fact that we have tended in recent times to neglect [the] deeper values in favor of our material strength. We have travelled in 100 years from the age of the pioneer to the age of payola."[5]

What has happened to us? Have we given up our old values because we are afraid of involvement with the problems of others? Do we keep our eyes, minds and hearts shut because we feel impotent in a mass society, afraid that if we speak out against injustice we'll be misunderstood and called "kooks"? But isn't that what being a patriotic American really consists of—speaking the truth even when the vogue is untruth, refusing to compromise even when the pressures of the consensus are against us? And aren't these qualities more needed than ever—in the light of the problems we face both here at home and throughout the world?

How come America is no longer a model for other peoples, an inspiration for the world? How come other countries are looking elsewhere for understanding and moral leadership? Let's face it, folks, when our actions are in so many ways the opposite of our pious speeches, people are bound to regard us as liars and devious cheats. So when we speak of peace in Vietnam and yet refuse to look into an offer of negotiations because of an impending election, people think twice about our sincerity. When we talk about helping the people of Vietnam and then haphazardly burn rice and strew the countryside with bombs, the rest of the world laughs through their tears. How much longer can we refuse to become outraged by the slaughter of innocent people? What has happened to our much-touted morality, our national ideals, and our religious commitments? I refuse to believe that there are no more Americans left. I can't believe that the

[5] Gerald Gardner, ed., *The Quotable Mr. Kennedy*, Popular Library, 1961, p. 10.

honest concern for human worth is gone forever as a part of the American character. Am I wrong? Have we all become so callous that even the sight of a pregnant woman burned by napalm doesn't cause us pain and make us want to put an end to war?

My dad died a year and a half ago. The agony and pain of his death for those of us close to him were difficult to bear, and I wish that no one would have to experience that sorrow unnecessarily. He was only one, yet so many people suffer because he is gone. War kills many unreasonably and the suffering is multiplied numerically and also because of the futility of it all. My whole being rebels against lifting a weapon to inflict that agony on another. I don't understand how anyone who has personally witnessed death could possibly want to make anyone else experience that distress. Can't we sincerely look upon all the peoples of the world as our brothers, and attempt to work out our problems without resorting to military power? That would be in keeping with another set of ideals that are supposedly basic to America; peace, honor and justice, with the use of force only as a last resort.

Yet how far we have moved from that ideal of a peaceful world! It seems that we as a nation have lost confidence in our way of life and so must resort to military power whenever we feel even slightly threatened. So when our government suspects that Communists (only fifty-five of them) are involved in a revolt in the Dominican Republic, we openly and with great pride send in thousands of troops to squelch an honest attempt to attain decent government. And look at Vietnam! As far as I am concerned the United States years ago assumed the role of an aggressor nation interfering in the internal affairs of another country which has been attempting to achieve unity and peace after decades of war. So now, even all the declarations stating that we would never initiate aggressive military action are proven false.

Are we going to accept these new redefinitions of what America is? Are we so afraid of what we are supposed to be? Are we so weak as a nation that we are no longer willing to take chances on our version of truth and perfection? Are we no longer going to be an example to the rest of the world of how people from all nations with different outlooks on life can live together harmoniously? If America is afraid to maintain its pioneer spirit, its lust for experimentation, its recognition of equality of all peoples, then she shall fail. We shall have proven that government of the people, by the people, for the people cannot survive.

And I, as an American, refuse to let that happen! I refuse to see an ideal that holds so much promise for mankind become shattered. I refuse to see a country that has offered so much to so many fade away into oblivion. No, America means too much to me to let a government destroy it. There is a difference between society and government. As Thomas Paine wrote in *Common Sense,* "Society is produced by our wants, and government by our wickedness; the former promotes our happiness positively by uniting our affections, the latter negatively by restraining our vices."[6] It is to that American society that I owe my allegiance, just as I am more personally concerned with what I am than with what someone tells me I am. I shall continue to pursue the dream, America, rather than follow the dictates of a government that is more concerned with short-range electoral gain or personal aggrandizement.

I hope that this view of America helps a little at least to explain the youth of today: those kids who took too seriously all that they were taught America was; those kids who saw parallels between their quest to become human, and the plight of their country and the world; those kids who are willing to go to jail for their belief in a world of equality and peace; those kids who seek understanding but can do without it.

For we are not afraid of our world, our government, abuse, or prison. We are pioneers again. We have a mission. We have a mission finally to make America the bastion of freedom, the arsenal of democracy, to make the world a place of brotherhood and peace. So we will continue to demonstrate against the war in Vietnam, in support of civil rights, in defense of freedom of speech. We will continue to discuss with anyone who will talk to us our government's policies and our own actions. Though we know that we were put on this earth for no reason but to live, we have made ethical human choices to involve ourselves in the affairs of the world. We have chosen not to be afraid to regard the people of Vietnam as our

[6] *Writing of Thomas Paine,* New York, Carlton House, p. 1.

brothers. And we have seen that people in Selma are no different than we are and should have the same opportunities for fulfillment as we.

Some of us have stopped marching and are looking for other ways to be effective in moving the world one step further toward a utopia envisioned by our forefathers almost two hundred years ago. What those ways will be we are still struggling with, for trying to find an individual way of coping with the world is difficult. But we will never turn back. We have seen what we can do, what ordinary human beings, no different than you who read or hear this, can do. Yes, we are not afraid, for we know that we have nothing to fear but fear itself.

So this is what I wanted to get off my chest. Yet I cannot conclude without issuing an invitation. I hope that I will have contributed at least a little to a deepening of understanding among the different generations of Americans, and that this will have been only a beginning. Let us start a national dialogue about the meaning of life. Let us talk together to try to bridge the remaining gaps between us, to help one another to overcome our respective fears. For only by doing so can we develop a united community that is committed to peace and progress. Through the understanding we could gain by such an open and mutually respecting encounter we all could then truly live and let live.

The Function of Insight

JOHN ROBERTSON*

MY college career began on a small campus of fewer than nine hundred students, in a small community of fewer than twenty-five thousand people. Though I remember feeling quite alone and anxious at first, I readily became part of what I would now describe as the typical college experience. I played games, sang songs, engaged in snow fights, and studied in my spare time.

As I look back on my freshman year I think that the greatest mistake I made was to put too great a value on belonging. The social environment in which I found myself was especially conducive to this type of error, being dominated by competitive living groups. For the sake of security I paid the price of knowing few people and having only one close friend. I remember marveling at the fact that out of 150 freshmen boys I should have been assigned to room with the one who turned out to be my best friend. With this convenient arrangement I proceeded to convince myself that any other friendships were not worth cultivating. When summer came and I left school I had many pleasant experiences to remember but I still knew but one person more than casually.

One might say that this is not a very severe criticism to make of myself, since most people have only a few intimate friends and many acquaintances. But the point is that close friends should not be a substitute for meaningful encounters with a wide variety of persons.

* *John Robertson, age twenty-four, graduated in Engineering from the University of California at Berkeley and is currently doing graduate work in Social Science at San Francisco State College. He plans to teach secondary school for a few years and then go on to get a Ph.D. in Education.*

To be able to open up to other people without first having to be sure of their commitment to oneself, is an ability I have since decided is well worth cultivating. Only with such an undemanding attitude is one free to understand other points of view, and in the broadest sense, those "other points of view" are what I think college is for. At that time of my life, however, I was unprepared to enter relationships that would not help to secure my self-confidence against a somewhat strange and perplexing world. As a result, my personal growth remained rather limited. I do not know what would have happened had I returned to this school in the fall—whether my previous habits would have been reinforced or if I would have become sure enough of myself to venture into broader and more challenging encounters. In any event, the following year found me enrolled at the University of California in Berkeley.

I had taken a liberal arts curriculum the year before with the thought of going on what was called a three-two plan, a plan whereby I would take three years of liberal arts and two of engineering and end up with a degree in both areas. At Berkeley, however, the situation demanded a decision between liberal arts or the college of engineering. The criterion I invoked, that of tangibility and practicability, pointed to the latter; so engineering was my choice. I remember that my impression of the social sciences and humanities was that the knowledge of the former was always uncertain and conjectural and that the latter required an individual capable of complete dedication and endowed with considerable talent. As it was, engineering suited my purpose quite well. The material in an engineering course follows a logical process of presentation. Most courses were complete in themselves or at most relied on clear-cut prerequisites. It was possible to establish well-defined goals and judge progress accordingly. Answers were either right or wrong, and if they were wrong it was simply a matter of finding out how to get the right one. I by no means want to imply that I regarded engineering as simple; on the contrary, for the average student to do well required considerable effort and commitment.

Toward the end of my junior year my values and general orientation to life began to undergo a significant change. Probably what happened to me was an experience common to many people as they mature a little. Stimulated by my contact with a knowledgeable and understanding friend, I began to broaden my intellectual horizons. Instead of dreading the liberal arts courses I had to take in engineering, I found myself reading philosophy, psychology and theology for pleasure, often at the expense of my engineering. This continued until my graduation from Cal, at which time I was anxious to take more nontechnical courses and hardly enthusiastic about embarking on an engineering career. I therefore decided to enroll at San Francisco State College, and took as diversified a curriculum as possible. Though this is an age when technology requires a high degree of specialization, I have become convinced that everyone needs first of all a good general education.

I now look back on my engineering curriculum at Berkeley with strongly critical feelings. It is now obvious to me that I was not really interested in my studies as I am now; they did not seem relevant in the way they do now. In other words, it *now* seems quite clear that I was never cut out to be an engineer. So I ask myself, whom do I blame for the four years that could have been spent more wisely? (It is a question, I might add, that is also of some interest to the taxpayer.)

In trying to answer this question I must examine both myself and the educational system of which I was a part. As far as I myself am concerned, the question I am most often asked is: Why did I change my mind so late? But this seems to me of only secondary importance. The more basic question I must ask myself is why I failed to make a personally more meaningful decision in the first place. And why was this? Possibly it was because I had never been shocked into confronting my own innate self. Possibly I am by nature a passive person who needs more external stimulation than others. Yet I somehow can't believe that I am alone. There are surely a great many people for whom the present educational system does not provide adequate occasions for a sufficiently searching investigation of their own potentialities.

Opportunities to get to know oneself are, of course, most limited of all in our typical engineering curricula. As has often been said, engineering programs are too exclusively concerned with professional training. I believe that the ideal way to remedy this would be to make engineering available only on a graduate level, after several years of more general educational preparation. The present shortcomings of engineering curricula might at least be mitigated if those who teach these courses made greater efforts to address themselves to their students as whole human beings. Yet here, too, I must be critical. It was my repeated experience that engineering instructors were precisely the kind of people whom one would expect the present system to produce. In other words, people educated in the ways of the system are returned as its instructors. It is a closed circle which makes for high technical competence but limited human and cultural perspectives.

While part of my error in majoring in engineering undoubtedly resulted from my own lack of self-awareness, part of the blame must thus be attributed to the existing educational system itself. For isn't a conscious knowledge of alternatives presupposed in the notion of free choice? And how can one expect the average American eighteen-year-old, raised in the limited world of our middle-class culture, to make a wise, lifetime vocational choice?

Having by now somewhat enlarged my conception of education and decided to devote myself to some aspect of it as a career, I have been thinking more and more about three basic questions. What are the areas in which education is relevant to the unique problems faced by modern man? Can education facilitate the making of increasingly complex decisions that today confront the average person? And, can education liberate man from a bureaucratic environment that is ceaselessly trying to objectify him? To discuss these questions I must first examine our present social environment, the various ways of reacting to it, and the kinds of specific roles education might play.

Our rapidly changing, technological society seems to have been developing for the past hundred years and, in a more fundamental sense, for the past two millennia. The most obvious changes have occurred in the nature of our tools and in the new organizational forms we have evolved to utilize them. As a result of these developments, we in the United States have for some decades been moving into what one economic historian has termed an age of "high mass consumption."[1] At least potentially, that is, we possess the scientific

[1] W. W. Rostow, *The Stages of Economic Growth,* London, Cambridge University Press, 1960.

and technological know-how to eliminate scarcity in regard to everything the human organism needs to sustain itself. In the process, moreover, increased efficiency through automation has made it possible to feed, clothe and shelter ourselves with only a fraction of the time and effort required formerly. These same advances have, of course, also brought the creation of nuclear weapons and the resultant fear and tension that haunt our lives. And as if to compensate for the increased possibility of death by war, medical science has progressed far toward eradicating the most deadly diseases.

Corresponding important changes have occurred in our attitudes toward life. We seem to be undergoing a time of deep-rooted intellectual and ethical ferment. Our traditional world view appears in many ways to have exhausted its potential for providing us with a viable orientation both to nature and other people. This older philosophy that I believe is today being outgrown I associate with the United States during the period it developed from an agrarian to an industrial society. Without wishing to imply any negative connotation, I would call the predominant outlook of this era materialistic. People were judged in terms of the things they possessed. It was as important for nations to strive after industrial pre-eminence as it was for people to acquire the goods industry produced. Being well thought of by one's fellowman was desirable, but one didn't need to bother about it too much, since it would surely result from a successful business career. People tended to be what David Riesman has called "inner-directed,"[2] in the sense that most of their values and goals became part of their personalities at an early age and remained relatively unchanged from then on. It also became customary for people to think in terms of depersonalized groups. Laborers and managers, the rich and the poor, foreigners and natives, were common descriptive categories. It was a time when most human relationships were economically and socially competitive, a time of sharp class distinctions. Also characteristic of the period was a certain naïveté regarding international relations, afforded us by our physical isolation from other countries. We were "morally virtuous" created by "divine destiny," and happy to give advice to whomever we considered less industrious than ourselves. In summary, the pervasive preoccupation

[2] David Riesman, *The Lonely Crowd,* New Haven, Yale University Press, 1950.

of this earlier era in our history was with the mastery of physical things, and people were rated in terms of their visible achievements in regard to that process.

The philosophy and discipline of materialistic development have made possible a measure of control over nature and standards of living unmatched in history. Yet these happy results have not been without a price. For while an industrially based market economy may be efficient from the point of view of the production and distribution of goods and services, it certainly does not acknowledge all our dimensions as human beings. To experience life and judge people chiefly in terms of such a scheme of values is therefore bound to result in what has come to be called alienation, from oneself as well as from others.

As heirs to the historical period of scientific and industrial dynamism, we face several kinds of problems. To some extent we are still afflicted by the fragmentation and alienation that seem endemic to this kind of developmental process. In addition, we are confronted by the ever increasing complexity that results from our technological achievements, high living standards, and geographical and social mobility. And beyond that, we are experiencing the uncertainties of abandoning much of our traditional world view and groping for another that will somehow enable us to live more fully.

How, in this situation of changing circumstances and frequently conflicting values, does one act as a moral person? How does one make coherent sense of it all and relate oneself to it in one's day-to-day living? As I see it, there are three possible ways to cope with this problem. One is to let oneself be guided by whim, so to speak. React the way you feel at the moment, whether it is consistent with past behavior or not. The second is to accept some ethical code and then act according to it whether it fits or not. And the final way is somehow to bridge the gap between one's ideas and realities and to become intellectually and experientially at one with oneself. The person who evolves such a response to life also acts ethically. But his ethical notions are so broadly human and adaptable that they can become part of his very nature and be applied almost intuitively and in a manner appropriate to every occasion. Such a person's actions are then essentially spontaneous. Yet if he is challenged, he is able to reassure himself and explain to others that his actions do in fact express a coherent set of beliefs and ethical commitments.

But do such spontaneous and intuitively ethical people need to reflect on their acts at all? Can't a person live fully and responsibly without having to be able to explain in words why certain actions are good and desirable, and others not? I am afraid that at our present juncture in history totally spontaneous and at the same time wise and moral behavior is impossible. While a flexible ethical commitment and the clues of everyday life can go a long way toward spontaneously orienting behavior, I believe that no one can dispense with thinking about their actions altogether. Even the most emancipated of us is still bound to be caught up in the rigidities of our traditional ethical assumptions in some measure. And the society in which we live is simply too complex and replete with situations involving value choices for a person to be able to get along without any reflective introspection whatever.

I know of two possible sources of sustaining orientation by which one's reflections and choices can be guided. Both require the person to transcend his immediate cultural conditioning and to try to confront life both more individually and universally. The one orientation is that of faith. The other is that of intellectual awareness or, as the philosopher Whitehead calls it, insight.[3] Of the two, faith is by far the more desirable. For while insight tends to lead only to a cerebral and analytical appreciation of life, faith is able to order the experiencing of our existence in its full, intuitive richness. Yet even though it is more limited, intellectual awareness can perform a vital function. It can enable us to make some sense out of our lives and so preserve our individual integrity while we search for a faith that will once again be satisfying and workable.

Since intellectual awareness operates through concepts and theories, there is of course always the danger that we may become so engrossed in our intellectualizing that we lose touch with the living realities we are trying to understand. The only defense against this is continuously to return to our direct, undifferentiated experiences, no matter how disruptive of our neat intellectual exercises this may

[3] Alfred North Whitehead, *Adventures of Ideas,* New York, Mentor Books, 1960.

prove. Such a return to firsthand experience as a corrective to our insight is not only necessary to keep our intellectual awareness practically relevant. It is nowadays insisted upon by students who refuse to accept academic analyses unless they find them meaningful in terms of their own personal concerns. The reason for this is that many of today's young people are engaged in what ultimately amounts to a religious quest. They are exploring themselves and the world with a view to developing new personal and social meanings. And this is why so much currrent unrest centers in our institutions of higher learning. These formally represent the quest for intellectual awareness. And if they are prepared to incorporate occasions that enable students to relate what they are learning to their own immediate experiences, they can also facilitate going beyond insight to the development of a larger and more inclusive faith.

Among my acquaintances I have observed three basic adjustments to today's world. The most unappealing of these is what I shall call the "unquestioning" approach. It would be too much to term this a philosophy, for it is in fact the very antithesis of the kind of understanding through reason and reflection at which philosophy aims. The distinguishing characteristic of the person who follows this formula is his willingness to accept his society as presently constituted without question and to take its human and moral adequacy for granted. People who operate in this manner are by no means lazy; they are often born gamesmen who devote tireless hours to learning the rules of the social game and how to break them with impunity. Their unconscious assumption is simply that whatever "pays off" in terms of existing social values is thereby an unqualified good.

But to justify such a psychologically and morally undiscriminating attitude one would have to take an entirely relativistic position and maintain that one set of values is as good as any other. And I do not believe this is so. Values *can* be judged, both with reference to basic human needs and in regard to particular historical circumstances. Some values facilitate human nature more fully and effectively than others. Some values are more appropriate in one kind of technological, social or political situation than others. In our present ethical ferment, for example, there are a great many philosophies of life we could follow. Take only such famous figures as Marx, Freud and

Sartre. Each of these offers his own interpretation of the world and recommends a different course of action. The implications of their ideas and ideals are significantly different. How, then, are we to make a judgment as to whose explanations and values are best, that is, most likely to prove viable and satisfying? We can do so only by subjecting them—and all ideas and ideals generally—to critical investigation.

On college campuses the unquestioning attitude is expressed most typically by the students who are out to beat the system. Their goal is not to think about themselves and their society but merely to acquire an academic degree. They are not interested in what can truly be called education. Their purpose is only to pass the formal requirements that will give them access to the social and material benefits for which the possession of an academic degree has come to be insisted upon. The social life of such students is dominated by considerations of prestige and status, and whatever surplus energy they have is poured into the pursuit of good times. I do not object to these entertainments in themselves. They are unhealthful only when they are not balanced by a serious side of life. That this kind of existence is today not altogether complete and satisfying is somewhat corroborated by the reactions of such students to the Berkeley Free Speech Movement. During this challenge to the morality of the Establishment, these merely career-minded people kept themselves entirely separate from the dialogue. It was not that they could not be heard, since arrangements existed to accommodate speakers representing all sides of the issue. But rather than engaging in discussion, these people threw garbage at those who did. Such actions seem to me to express deep-seated hostilities, not in the first instance toward the Berkeley rebels but against their own unsatisfying way of life which the Free Speech Movement unwittingly put into question.

The second basic attitude I see among my contemporaries is what I would call the "cynical" approach. It succeeds where the unquestioning attitude fails, but is unacceptable to me for other reasons. It has questioned several or all traditional American values and found them in many ways lacking. But it does not go on from there to search for more suitable patterns of living to replace or supplement those which are found wanting. It is above all a reaction against hypocrisy, and as such it can indeed point to many inconsistencies in our preachments and practices. Our alleged adherence to Christian ethics, our vaunted devotion to peace and the self-determination of peoples, our much-paraded enlightenment on the subject of sex—all are in many ways given the lie by the ways we actually live. Being the overstated ideals they are, they understandably evoke disillusionment. Yet whether this disillusionment justifies giving up on our society altogether is another matter. To me, at least, it does not.

Since I concede many of the points which those who take the cynical view make, I have no easy answer with which to oppose them. Probably the differences between their conclusions and my own are in the last analysis a matter of temperament. Certain personality types react to disillusionment more bitterly than others. I suspect that those who do, thereby give indication that they are suffering from psychological problems that may best be solved on an individual basis. In any event, someone who chooses to reject the possibility of positive action colors the way he sees life from then on. He puts himself beyond the reach of arguments to the contrary because his most fundamental premise is negative. To change he must have new experiences, not another argument.

The final pattern of behavior I have observed among my fellow students is one by which I have been strongly tempted myself. I shall refer to it by Eric Hoffer's term as that of the "true believer."[4] For two and a half of the four years I spent at Berkeley, most of my energies were devoted to engineering. Even so, my studies did not fill me with any great enthusiasm. I believe in retrospect that I longed all the while for somone or something to become really excited about. I would like to have had a cause and remember envying those who did—whether it was civil rights, free speech, anti-Communism, anti-capitalism, or any of the numerous others that were available. But here was my greatest problem: since there are at least two sides to every issue, and since each side is equally dedicated and capable of arguing its case, I could never make a choice. Perhaps if belonging to a group had not seemed to demand such total allegiance, the decision to commit myself might have been easier; but on the other hand, it would also have lost some of its attractiveness.

I think that what most basically troubles me about the "true

[4] Eric Hoffer, *The True Believer,* New York, Mentor Books, 1961.

believer" approach is that it attracts certain personality types who are inclined not to do justice to the complexity of the issues involved. To achieve a feeling of certainty worthy of total dedication, such people are often prepared dangerously to oversimplify problems and solutions. While I cannot, therefore, follow their example, I must point out that when guided by strong, responsible and perceptive leaders, people with this type of personality and orientation to life can play an important part in working toward positive social goals.

Being by disposition and outlook prevented from adopting any of the main attitudes that appear to satisfy many of my contemporaries, I find myself in a rather individual and detached position. All I can fall back on are some very general guiding principles: first, that it is essential to care about life, to try to understand it, and to maintain some mindfulness of its complexities; and second, that some form of action is necessary—even at the risk of acting on the basis of incomplete knowledge and thus failing to achieve one's original objectives. Beyond these principles, I believe with the psychologist and philosopher C. G. Jung that modern man needs essentially four things: faith, hope, love and insight.[5] That is why I am concerned with education. For though education is not the whole answer, it can make a vital contribution at least to the development of insight. While the unquestioning, the cynics and the true believers reject insight as either too threatening or too cautious, I myself am convinced that it today provides our most reliable creative instrument.

And how can education best serve the development of insight? Most importantly, it must cultivate a spirit of inquiry. It must do so by encouraging people to build meaningful bridges between their own personal processes and events in the world at large. Once having triggered such personally rooted intellectual curiosity, education must nourish, structure and at the same time free it so that it can penetrate human experiences as deeply as our faculties make possible. To accomplish this task, education must bring to bear every perspective that human observation and imagination have made available. It must utilize the analyses of the various physical and social sciences. It must combine these with a continuous awareness of historical dimen-

[5] C. G. Jung, *Modern Man in Search of a Soul,* translated by W. S. Dell and C. F. Baynes, New York, Harcourt, Brace (Harvest), 1933.

sions. It must offer students opportunities to derive stimulation and meaning from the arts. It must permit them to pursue their studies in frank relationship to the practical problems and moral dilemmas they face in their own lives. And above all, it must recognize that effective education and hence the attainment of insight are ultimately very individual matters. While providing common frameworks and materials, it must invite everyone to think through his realities in his own ways. For only to the extent people achieve such personally meaningful insights will they be secure enough to go on to modern man's other three needs—faith, hope and love.

A Case for Humane Intelligence

MICHAEL O'NEIL*

ONE of the purposes of this collection of essays is to help persuade the American community to re-examine some of its conventional ideas about higher education. In addressing ourselves to this task we are thus making at least two assumptions. We believe that as presently conceived and constituted American higher education is not adequately meeting the challenges of today's evolving world. And we are assuming that if we convincingly demonstrate why and how American higher education ought to be altered, we will, in fact, make a difference. I personally share this faith—both in our ability to make a cogent case in this regard, and in our fellow citizens' willingness to give us a sympathetic hearing. In the course of my own essay, indeed, I will present a plea for the revitalization of faith in general.

Education cannot be considered apart from the society it expresses and serves—local, national, and today increasingly global. To talk meaningfully about American higher education one must therefore also concern onself with the nature of the contemporary world. And since this world is undergoing a major transition, one must examine the dominant trends that seem to be at work. These trends can be analyzed in many ways, but as I see it, they are most fundamentally twofold. The world is moving toward increasing centralization. And there is a universal striving for mankind's material betterment.

On the surface of it, global integration seems a remote prospect

* *Michael O'Neil, age twenty-four, is the son of a police officer in southern California. He has served three years in the U.S. Marine Corps and is presently a junior in Political Science. He plans to go to graduate school to study Far Eastern affairs.*

indeed. Intensely nationalistic forces appear to be pulling mankind further and further apart. Yet these forces, no matter how disruptive, are in fact responses to the very kinds of long-range cultural, economic and technological developments that in the end cannot but eliminate them. The centralizing process in our world is taking place almost completely below the level of our awareness. It is largely ignored by our newspapers, our public opinion, and even in the statements and actions of our political leaders. But its roots run deeply and someday it will sprout a tree hitherto seen only in the dreams—or nightmares—of men. For someday some kind of centralizing order and authority are going to have to cope effectively with irreversible changes in human aspirations and techniques that even now greatly affect the lives of people all over the globe. International order and mutual responsibility are clearly called for when a fluctuation on the New York Stock Exchange has world-wide economic repercussions, when a railway jam on Switzerland's St. Gotthard line backs up freight in Scandinavia, when mass communications take the story of Selma, Alabama, to Monrovia, West Africa, and when the industrially advanced nations have the know-how and resources to produce increasingly worrisome surpluses while much of the rest of the world remains on the edge of starvation.

Some interpreters of today's world claim that the trend of centralization is leading toward either a bipolar mobilization of whites versus coloreds, of haves versus have-nots, or of one ideological bloc against another. But these are not realistic alternatives. The logic of contemporary socioeconomic ideas, industrial techniques and military weapons requires nothing less than global world order. Either sovereign nation states are dead or mankind is dead.

I suggested that the second main trend in today's world is the universal drive for material betterment. I realize that there is currently more talk of raising physical standards than there are tangible results in that direction. The gap between rich and poor nations has, in fact, been increasing. Yet even though it suffers temporary setbacks, the battle for a decent standard of living for all peoples cannot be halted. The hearts and minds of human beings everywhere are set on it. In the short run, the frustrations that this quest engenders are bound to be highly explosive. But eventually it is certain to be accomplished. For where there is all this will, it is unthinkable that there is not going to be found a way.

Given these trends, the key questions facing contemporary man concern what *kind* of world order he is going to build, and what he is going to do with himself as *more* than a mere physical organism. On the answers he works out for these questions hangs the future not necessarily of life, but certainly of what we call civilization. And for these answers, we are ourselves responsible.

There are many who claim that science is incompatible with the idea of free will. Perhaps such a view seemed plausible in the past. But it certainly is not today. For today science and technology not only are satisfied to coexist with the notion of free will; their high degree of development and the powers they have unleashed make it absolutely essential that we subscribe to the precepts of free will and personal responsibility. The frontiers of science are theoretically unlimited. Whereas natural catastrophes, disease and starvation were once fatalistically accepted, science and technology now strongly indicate that there will be a day when nothing in the physical life of man, not even death, will be inevitable. We are truly becoming the masters of our physical fate. If we do not soon solve our physical problems, it will be because of our own stupidity and wickedness, not because we do not have the opportunity. Can we intelligently apply the unprecedented knowledge at our command? Can we place it in the service of the ideals of human worth, brotherhood and dignity? Or will we misuse it merely to exploit and manipulate one another?

The trends and circumstances which are reshaping today's world are so vast and complex that in their presence man often stands confused and troubled. He asks questions which his traditional concepts and institutions can no longer answer. In such a transitional world of troubled man, there is great danger that the forces of our age will become the tools of those who want to use their fellows for their own cause or profit. For taken together, our widespread uncertainties along with the nature of today's technology and psychological skills constitute a greater potential for human enslavement than has ever before existed.

At the root of the contemporary threat to our freedom is a very old and much-used conception of man. It is the misanthropic idea that human beings are innately too selfish, stupid, belligerent and divided to willingly join together in mutual advantage and harmony. Applied to today, this Hobbesian argument maintains that the world has become so crowded and complex that men can no longer be effectively coordinated save through some kind of systematic coercion.

Opposed to the pessimistic view of man and its accompanying threat to his freedom is a dynamic conception of the practicability of libertarian and democratic ideals. It is a conception which strives to put in man's service the powers of our age. It is the belief that with these powers man can pull upward his society as he himself ascends. It is a conception which claims that man can remake his institutions and concepts in such a way that they will shape a humane world order.

Above all, the conception of libertarian and democratic ideals is an expression of faith in man, a faith based not on the dictates of an authority or majority but in the creative potentialities of man himself. It is the belief that if you put faith in man, man will be deserving of this faith and will justify it in practice. It is analogous to the faith that underlies scientific research.

To paraphrase and grossly oversimplify the philosopher of science Charles Sanders Peirce,[1] scientific inquiry, because of man's human limitations, cannot properly start with a priori notions of Truth. That is, because man is not one and the same with the Real, he cannot know Reality. However, to start scientific research, man, whether he realizes and admits it or not, must believe that there *is* a Reality and that it is regular. Otherwise, inquiry is futile; and, indeed, as Jean Paul Sartre tell us, life itself is then absurd. Our best scientists, while not knowing the Real, have nevertheless believed in its existence. And for this reason they have found much of that small part of Reality which we *can* know—namely, the shared opinion of what are conceivable practical consequences in our experiential realm of living. On the basis of their faith, and because of a willingness to constantly test their beliefs or hypotheses about Reality, scientists have, for example, launched Mariner IV.

The conclusion to be drawn here concerns the logical imperative of

[1] Charles Sanders Peirce, *Essays in the Philosophy of Science,* New York, Bobbs-Merrill, 1957.

faith. In science we have believed, and hence we have achieved. What now remains is to extend logical faith beyond science. We need to humbly recognize that man has not yet been seen in the fullness of his being, that there is a Reality about him which has so far escaped us. In order to develop the potentialities of man, we must put faith in man. To launch mankind's beauty and creativity, we must believe in him and be willing to work by trial and error toward his ever greater improvement. We can best do this by constantly improving the implementation of democratic and libertarian ideals. And to effectively implement these ideals, we must develop a practical dedication to them which is as deep as is our dedication to the scientific method.

I do not define libertarian and democratic ideals in accordance with any ideology. I define them experientially. That is, I mean by them those concepts and practices which further the development and realization of the faith in man which underlies them. Thus, for example, the proposal to institute world peace by subjugating man to a coercively ordered world society is anathema to libertarian and democratic ideals; for, to name only a few of its gross faults, it admits lack of faith in the potential for ever higher good in mankind; it repels the logic of man's opportunity to participate in the building of an ever greater society; and it refutes the plainly indicated potential of truly free men.

If the forces of our age are put in the service of man, and, directly related to this, if libertarian and democratic ideals are made the guiding principles of the future one world, mankind will enter an unprecedented age of humaneness, abundance, and peace. However, such a world society is a questionable aspect of our future. Its development is dependent upon that more-than-material betterment of man which I earlier mentioned.

Both prerequisite and supplementary to continuous progress toward a humane world order is what I shall call the development of metatelic values and aspirations. I refer to man's need for a conception of human perfectness that is so open-ended, self-transcending and dynamically formative that it can never be claimed to have been fully realized. I mean an abstract, limitless ideal of human potentialities which can serve man as his ultimate inspiration and which he will feel impelled always to redefine and more fully to actualize as he moves from one successful experience to another. I believe such an ideal inspiration and reference for human strivings is essential for two reasons. It implies that no existing set of objectives and arrangements is ever finally sufficient. And it thereby provides a thrust to human unfolding that transcends the cultural expectations of any particular situation. By virtue of this fact, it also provides justification for the libertarian and democratic ideals of which I have spoken. And it at the same time requires that man operate in terms of these ideals if the never-consummated search for his full being is to be possible.

Unfortunately, we live in an age when faith both in the instrumental ideals of liberty and democracy and in the more abstract notion of infinite human perfectability is neither strong nor widespread. Faith of any kind—in the abstract, in ideals, in man himself—is badly languishing. Nor is our current anti-faith the rational, faith-inspired and creative reaction against dogmatism that earlier in Western history produced many of mankind's greatest moments. Instead, it is an expression of normlessness, confusion, despair, and extreme fear—fear of self, fear of the future, fear of all life. It is a rationalization for inactivity, for failure to sacrifice and plan, for failure to dream. It is rooted in more than the death of *a* God; it stems from the belief that "God is dead" and that no metaphysical orientation is possible or permissible. It is the reason contemporary man finds it so difficult to make moral choices and formulate clear purposes. Contemporary anti-faith is the reason modern man, when not standing inert, is reaching committee-type decisions with his psychiatrist, or finding direction in a bottle of liquor, tranquilizers or pep pills.

We cannot long endure the highly demoralized state which results from anti-faith. This is the major threat to our future in one world. If man too long lives in mental, moral, and social chaos, he inevitably turns to irrational faith. He turns to faith in extremist leaders, material success, scientism, or some other "ism" which, because it eliminates faith in man, leads to tyranny. This is to say that mankind is entirely capable of enslaving himself, of voluntarily committing himself to the collective security, order, and purpose of a tyrannical world state. And given the forces of our age, I am saying that we are entirely capable of developing ourselves into a race of human automatons, eugenically shaped, bureaucratically organized, technologically brainwashed, scientifically coerced, and completely subservient to a pseudo divine collective.

If the foregoing view is correct, it is clear that our most urgent task is the rebuilding of man's faith in man. Yet this is bound to be a most difficult undertaking. We cannot hope to create the kind of faith in man I am talking about overnight. At least for the time being we must work toward this objective indirectly—by demonstrating to all men everywhere the practical and personal benefits of liberalism and democracy. It must be shown what liberal and democratic institutions can do—that they provide the best possible answer to man's need for a coordinating social principle and that they therefore best facilitate his quest freely to participate in the shaping of his own destiny.

Despite all her shortcomings, I believe that the role of demonstrator in the task of restoring faith in man through the effective practice of liberalism and democracy falls to the United States. America commands the greatest force, power and influence in the world today. Also, at least in principle if not always in practice, the United States remains the world's most libertarian and democratic country. It is therefore America's opportunity and duty to exemplify to the world dynamic actualizations of libertarian and democratic ideals. Unless the United States assumes this duty, all that is humane and promising about this country will be lost. America, the idea, will perish.

To call on America for world involvement is not to call on her for world crusade. One does not spread ideals and institutions by exporting economic exploitation and armies. We must give up our obsession with force and power. We must be self-confident enough to enter into relationships on all levels with all peoples, currently friends or foes; and, even more important, after exemplifying the self-evident advantages of our ideals, and while yet engaged in the continuing development of these ideals at home, we Americans must be intelligent enough to realize that all peoples must be free to interpret and institute faith in mankind in accordance with their own indigenous circumstances and values. We must, then, be dedicated not to universally instituting our specific way of life, but to sharing with all the ideals which underlie our way of life.

To be an international exemplar, America must undergo reform at home. Our country has too long held on to outworn and even erroneous ideas which no longer, if ever they did, serve libertarian and democratic ideals. We have too long believed that irresponsible self-interests would automatically produce a progressive, harmonious society. We have relied on a mechanistically conceived market which, even if it ever did promote goods, always ignored men. We have practiced an amoral, anti-leadership politics which has too often responded to conflicting special interests and too seldom to community needs. By moral and intellectual default, we have allowed injustice and poverty to survive in our very midst.

Because many of the concepts by which we are guided have become outdated (if they ever were humanly appropriate), we face an unprecedented challenge to our highest faculty, our creative reason. Whereas in the past we have needed mainly our backs, hands, and practical good sense, today, more than anything else, we must call upon our powers to think penetratingly and imaginatively. To understand and guide the vast forces transforming today's world, to map out our new possibilities and goals, to implement a dynamic conception of libertarian and democratic ideals—to respond to these tremendous challenges we must bring to bear every bit of constructive intelligence we can muster. All our ideas and institutions must be honestly and critically evaluated and all of them must pass the test of appropriateness and, where necessary, be updated or replaced.

The task of providing this infusion of critical and creative reason cannot but fall mainly to our intellectual centers, our American colleges and universities. Of all our institutions, the one that holds the greatest promise and faces the greatest challenges is higher education. It is hardly too much to say that the future of the world depends in important measure on the kind of influences upon American society that can emanate from our colleges and universities.

America is today experiencing an educational revolution. One of the two main aspects of this revolution is the increasingly pivotal role being played by our institutions of higher learning in furnishing the scientific and organizational know-how to operate our industrially based, mass society. America is today turning its higher education into a knowledge industry that is becoming the fulcrum of its national growth. The chief reason for this is that the technical and organizational problems we face are too large and complex to be dealt with by uncoordinated conferences, isolated surveys, governmental studies, and individual research projects. What is needed instead are cooperative, planned syntheses of knowledge and expertise from a wide range of disciplines, which must then be focused on specific problems. And it is mainly by our colleges and universities that this service is being provided. It today constitutes the principal source of their status with the general public and accounts for the biggest portion of their financing.

The other major aspect of America's current educational revolution lies in the fact that more and more of our people are going to college. As one of the consequences of this, almost all of our future leaders—as well as the people who elect them—will have experienced higher education. This means that the quality of their response to our society's problems will depend in large measure on the quality of the education that our colleges and universities have been able to provide them.

It goes without saying that we must make higher education as effective in preparing us for this philosophical and political function as we can. *America's higher learning must concern itself with the continuous redevelopment of ideas, values and institutions which are applicable to our ever changing conditions and inspired by the faith in mankind that underlies liberalism and democracy.* I would call this a third major aspect of our educational revolution. To date, however, this further function of higher education is on the whole little recognized. And it is seriously endangered by the other two developments I have cited—by the development of our colleges and universities into centers of operational know-how, and by their absorption in the job of educating ever greater numbers.

In itself, the application of knowledge for the more efficient operation of our society through our colleges and universities is undoubtedly a good thing. Yet it must be recognized that to provide expertise is not the same thing as significantly to evaluate and alter. That is, it is not adequately to meet the total challenge that education today faces. Moreover, these two distinct functions require different kinds of people and organizations. One cannot expect a force whose business is to help run a system, at the same time also to question its basic assumptions. Indeed, as has become increasingly evident, the more energies our colleges and universities have devoted to solving our society's technical problems, the less they have been concerned with evaluating and recreating its foundations.

The ever larger numbers being handled by our institutions of higher learning also retard the development of the creative function of education. While mass education is certainly a worthy ideal, it is not a sufficient educational achievement by itself. Since many students continue to attend college for economically and socially "practical" reasons, the function of mass education in effect converges with that of servicing the society with expertise. It is then these simultaneous and mutually reinforcing activities that tend to make American institutions of higher learning into the businesslike treadmills whose biggest net contribution is to perpetuate the status quo.

It seems to me a first precondition for the fundamental re-evaluation of our society's current directions that what I am calling the purely educational function of colleges and universities and their role as institutions for specialized training be organizationally separated. Our graduate and professional schools could then be oriented to turning out experts, not claiming at the same time also to be concerned with education in the traditional humanistic sense. And our undergraduate schools could devote themselves to pure education, without feeling it necessary to seek status and financing by pretending to be doing more than that—as is all too often the case at present.

If we utilize our undergraduate schools for general education and creative thinking, and if we gear our graduate and professional schools for training people in the mastery of our physical environment, we would only be taking a further step in a trend already in progress. We would be admitting and coping with the fact that our graduate and professional schools have more and more become training grounds for business and government; that they have contributed very little by way of understanding of our civilization's total situation; and that with their emphasis on highly specialized academic research, they have in fact discouraged the many gifted people on their payrolls from concerning themselves with the new horizons and problems of our age as a whole.

Far too many of our educated people have no idea of the larger assumptions and implications of the expertises they practice. Having been trained in what in effect are vocational studies, they take the existence and morality of the status quo entirely for granted. To remedy this we must make certain that everyone is first exposed to a general education in the complexities of life in their full dimensions, and that during this educational experience they hear not only from expert scholars but also from teachers who will encourage them to think for themselves. Only after they have passed through this truly liberal phase of their education ought they to be admitted to graduate and professional schools. While the purpose of the undergraduate schools should thus be to help people educate themselves as human beings, the chief work of graduate and professional institutions should be to provide the intellectual tools for the society's day-to-day functioning. And contrary to what is now generally the case, the job of teaching and creative thinking should not be rated as any less important and prestigious than that of producing academic or scientific experts. For if anything, the concern with man's needs and life as a whole is a humanly more actualizing and dignifying activity than is the task of training him for specialized roles.

The actual establishment of the kind of division of labor between undergraduate and graduate learning that I am proposing would require a number of basic changes in both types of institutions. To list specific reforms for our graduate schools must fall to someone more qualified than I. At my present level of experience I feel I should confine myself to some of the alterations badly needed in our undergraduate education.

The ideal undergraduate college would not have a program of required courses. It would recognize that a highly structured curriculum is a sign of educational weakness. Its aim would be to help each student develop his individual potential rather than memorize information and work chiefly for grades. It would not conceive of the student's mind as a receptacle into which must be poured a certain volume of facts and figures. It would trust the student to decide for himself what is educationally relevant and what extracurricular activities are worth-while or not. With a basic faith in man, the ideal college would view the student's mind as something individually alive and would try to stimulate it and judge its performance according to its own unique dispositions.

The ideal undergraduate college would recognize that students come to it with their own innate gifts, needs and interests. It would accept and retain only those students who feel genuinely excited by intellectual activity, a criterion that has nothing at all to do with what is called "I.Q." And it would operate on the premise that if given enough time and if appropriately stimulated by their academic environment, most students can be counted on to find their own intellectual challenges and to pursue their studies with their own, self-imposed discipline.

There would be many more kinds of course offerings in the ideal undergraduate college. Especially emphasized would be courses in social and group processes as well as in the various arts—all areas of relevance for our changing and increasingly affluent society. And even more important than the expansion of the number of courses offered would be a radical alteration in the way they are taught and organized. The introductory course in biology, currently a very unpopular subject required at most colleges, provides a good example. In addition to the standard survey course which teaches a mass of biological definitions, the ideal college would offer another course which considers the personal and social implications of the biological knowledge presented and which traces the relationships of this knowledge to all other realms of human experience. All survey courses that concentrate on a mass of data, and all courses designed to force students to "appreciate" something or other, would be limited to future experts in those fields. Only future biologists, for example, would be required to learn a textbook-full of biological definitions. Other students would take a course designed to open to them the wonders that biology is exploring and to enable them to absorb these discoveries into their lives as a whole.

All survey courses in the ideal undergraduate college would be interdisciplinary. It would be realized that the ultimate subject of study is the whole human being in his total context and that every aspect of this subject is inseparably involved in every other. In place of today's one-year, specialized course in United States history, for example, the ideal college would offer a three- or four-year course in American civilization, a course which would bring together and transcend all conventional academic disciplines to present a unified, organic conception of America in its full dynamism and complexity.

As I mentioned earlier, today's teaching methods would be radically altered by the ideal undergraduate college. The teaching process would rely heavily upon dialogue between students and professors. Professors will have realized that straight lecturing quickly reaches a point of diminishing returns, that students can be talked at for only a limited span of time, and that they respond best when part of a barely organized, two-way conversation. Being a breeding ground for democratic methods, and posited on the libertarian faith in mankind, the ideal undergraduate college would provide continuous opportunity for teachers and students to cooperatively work out solutions both to academic questions and to the wider range of contemporary and perennial problems of human existence. This, far more than student government, will make students feel part of their education; this, far more than freshman orientation programs, will awaken their intellectual abilities; and this—a simple change in classroom procedure—will do more than any number of speeches by college deans and presidents to overcome the common view among today's students that college means impersonality, futility, intellectual suffocation, and bureaucratic regimentation.

To help make students free to learn, the ideal undergraduate college will have abolished the grading system. It will have realized that the highly competitive grading system of today is detrimental to learning; that it focuses students' attention on grades and not on knowledge; that it too often rewards those regimented students who perfectly distribute their time and effort over a wide, shallow area to produce a good grade point average, and not often enough those creative few who get thoroughly wrapped up in one or two courses. It will have realized that the grading system too often rewards those students who unquestioningly accept the material presented to them as fact and who are intellectually cautious or indeed dead; and not often enough those students who think freely and independently, who deal with problems for which the answers are ambiguous or unknown, and who discover not answers, but new and greater questions. The ideal undergraduate college, then, would determine who stays and who leaves, and who goes to graduate school and who doesn't, and who graduates with honors and who doesn't, and who gets what kind of job recommendation, by means and measurements other than the traditional grading system. Once during each school year, and twice during the freshman year, all students would appear individually before a panel of faculty members. By submitting a written paper, research project or work of art, or by presenting himself orally, or by agreeing to take written examinations, or by any other reasonable means chosen by himself, the student would seek to convince the faculty panel that he has been using well the college's opportunities. Any means of testing that the student chooses would examine his understanding and insight, not his ability to regurgitate "factual" material.

Students would be encouraged to engage in independent research projects and studies. Indeed, entire semesters could be devoted to one wide-ranging and preferably interdisciplinary project or study.

Almost all classes would meet only once a week. This would enable students not only to read, but also to think about assignments before discussing them in class. Some formal class sessions would be canceled and the saved time would be used for scheduled, but informal, meetings between individual students and their professors. Teachers and students would be free not only to discuss the student's academic work, but also to let a spontaneous conversation wander freely.

Courses would be concerned much more with the caliber of the material covered and the quality of student work than with the quantity of either. Busy-work would be eliminated. Compared to today's undergraduate, tomorrow's student would read less, write less, and take fewer exams; but he would converse more, think more, understand more, create more, write better, and deal with far more sophisticated materials.

The ideal undergraduate college would be concerned with expanding man's knowledge of man, not with expanding man's mastery over other men. Existing in an age of intellectual crisis, it would realize that to develop man's mind, it must restore those powers of contemplation which have too long been greatly weakened by Western man's devotion to political, economic, and technological conquest. It would realize that in a quest for rather blind and pure power, we have lost sight of the ends of man, of what man is, of how he should live, and of how our various power achievements could and should serve him.

A major concern of the ideal undergraduate college would be that its graduates enter the world with guiding principles, with a general orientation to life. But despite this fact, the college would not try to force any specific principles upon its students. Instead, it would leave students free to develop their own values. Indeed, the ideal college would strongly encourage students to do so. It would point out to students that they do inevitably have values and that, therefore, they should always admit their presence, and always stand ready both to defend and change them. It would point out to students that failing to admit and practice values leads to a normlessness which inhibits full intellectual and moral development, and that unless one eventually proceeds with clear purposes and goals, he proceeds too long by a wasteful, frustrating, and self-destroying system of trial and error.

The ideal college would teach students that while learning how to think is very important, realizing for what they should think and why, is even more important. It would point out to students that too often pure, unguided reason is used to vanquish, dehumanize, and devour man. It would point out that a humane orientation to life must be more than one of pure reason, that true intelligence is a synthesis of purposes, values, emotions, and reason; and that, therefore, true intelligence is a system of deep and guiding intellectual beliefs. In helping students to develop their own intellectual beliefs, the ideal college would be preparing them to seek constant improvement of society, of mankind, and of themselves.

The ideal undergraduate college would strive to develop in its students a capacity for creativity. Rather than fearing those inner forces which are today very little understood and are called irrational and nonrational, the ideal college would see them as composing a realm of preconsciousness which can lead man to an intuitive knowledge very often more rational than the knowledge which is produced by a simple retracing of intellectual steps already taken. Furthermore, the ideal college would realize that to create is to expand one's mind and release one's inner energies in a constructive direction; and that, therefore, to create is to give one faith in mankind.

Although delightful to attend, the ideal undergraduate college would make exacting demands on its students. It would force them to see social reality not as something affording them justification for self-pity, but as a realm for great opportunity, challenge, and excitement. Even more important, students would be expected to push themselves to the limits of their own powers. The college would know that as society grows more complicated, increasingly stronger men are required to hold it together; and thus the college would practice not equality of education, but equality of educational opportunity for each individual to achieve as far as possible that personal intellectual excellence which this democracy must have from many men in order to survive. Students, then, would be forced to test themselves within themselves. But compared to the labor of today's student, tomorrow's would be far more pleasant; it would be exciting and indeed heroic. For instead of competing against his classmates, the system, and the grading scale, tomorrow's student would reach for the utmost development of his own potentialities. Occasionally, in the pursuit, he might even wreck himself upon something deserving of his effort.

I have established very high ideals for the undergraduate college of tomorrow. I have done this because one must set his ideals high in order to reach the level of bare necessity. I have done this because America must set her educational ideals high in order to stand a chance of surviving her present intellectual crisis. The American college must ask itself what kind of world can be, what kind of world it wants to help build, and how it can best do so. The American college must clearly formulate our world's problems and then it must find, test, develop, and apply solutions. It must send to the world's leadership posts truly educated, not just trained, men. And, of course, to adequately do all this, it must constantly strive to perfect the internal actualizations of its own democratic and libertarian ideals.

Past generations of Westerners and Americans have given the Americans of our generation the blind powers we need in order to fulfill our opportunity to help build that humane world order which is now required. To respond successfully to that opportunity is the tremendous challenge of our generation. If the colleges fail, we all will fail. And if all fail, a humane one world will not materialize, and civilization, both as we've known and envisioned it, will fall.

Challenges are not new in human history. All generations have been required to meet the crisis of their age, and, of course, some generations have met their requirements more effectively than others.

Thus it is not true that our age is faced with the crisis of mankind. It is faced with *a* crisis. However, it is true that our age is challenged to an extent never exceeded and rarely equaled, in mankind's life on this planet. And it is also true that in order to successfully meet our challenge, man's mind, more than ever before, must reign supreme.

To the American colleges and universities has fallen the task of playing the world's most significant part in making man's mind supreme. Western civilization has already deeply touched the lives of nearly all the peoples of the earth. America is already a world leader in possession of great powers. Therefore, as civilizations before us, we can, if we complement our power with an overriding intellectual development, become the foremost cultural influence of the emerging world. Out of the ferment of Hellenic Greece came some of Western civilization's most important roots. Out of the ferment of twentieth-century America can come some of the ethical and cosmological visions so essential for the shaping of our evolving global civilization. We need but make humane intelligence supreme in our own country to help make it supreme in the coming world order. The opportunity and responsibility are ours; for our own sake and for the sake of mankind—past, present and future.

I should conclude these thoughts about education in the context of America and the world at large with at least a few words about my own personal relationship to what I have said. I have served three years and nine months in this country's Marine Corps. I believe I served well. I was awarded military commendations. And I was proud to be a member of a force that has played such an important part in meeting some of the *external* threats to this nation and the promise that it has historically represented. From 1959 until 1963 I saw no contradiction between my ideals and military service. But it is now 1966. My country is part of a nightmare as old as man, and thus so am I. I see it as my duty to help abolish that nightmare. And as I now more fully understand it, this cannot be accomplished through the use of military force. Not only does the intrusion of force into today's infinitely complex and deeply felt human developments fail to reach the springs of people's actions. It also cannot but damage the quest for a common, universal human purpose that is the unique opportunity and imperative of our age. More than that, the preoccupation with force leads to an aggravation and mobilization of our anxieties, causes us to regress to a myopic nationalism, and so diverts us both from the great promise of today's world and from the inescapable problems that must be faced if that promise is to be made a reality. It is to that promise that I will look in future for my inspiration. And it is to the analysis and solution of the problems involved in its actualization—problems requiring above all what I have called the application of humane intelligence—that I hope to devote my energies.

Bob Dylan, Erich Fromm and Beyond: A Look at the New Politics

DONNA MICKLESON*

THERE is a story told in the civil rights movement about a Negro with one leg who has worked both in the South and in Northern urban areas for some time. One day during a Chicago school demonstration in which boycotting school children joined civil rights workers and parents in blocking a main thoroughfare, an outraged little old lady, who apparently saw him as the most vulnerable link in the chain of bodies, stamped indignantly up to him and shouted, "Young man, just why are you doing this?" (As if he should have been gratefully working in a center for the handicapped at thirty-five cents an hour and praying for restitution of his lost limb.) In response, he whirled about and, pointing the crutch straight at her, replied accusingly, "Because *you* didn't buy enough Easter seals!"

There are times, like this one, when I feel the same sort of frustration this man must have felt in trying to answer, calmly and rationally, the continuing question: Why protest? For before it is possible to go on to the more difficult problems of how to protest effectively, and how to find out where positive alternatives lie, one must begin with the utterly fundamental question: Why? Just what is wrong?

I think there are essentially two main answers to that question. What is most obviously and urgently wrong concerns the large

* *Donna Mickleson, age twenty-three, has a B.A. in Political Science from San Francisco State College and is currently doing graduate work in English and Creative Writing at the same institution. She has been active in student government, civil rights and support of striking California farm workers. She plans to get a Ph.D. in English and to teach, write and remain active in community work.*

minority of Americans that shares neither in the great material benefits of this country nor in the making of its political decisions. For them the question is one of asking in. From the South comes the knock on the door of the voting booth. In the Northern urban centers it is the board of education, the city housing administration and the welfare office that are being asked to respond.

I spent a part of one summer in Washington, D.C., lobbying on behalf of the Mississippi Freedom Democratic party (FDP). Four native Negro Mississippians sought election to Congressional seats long held by die-hard white segregationists. At every step of the way, from the registrars' offices in their home counties to the 1964 Democratic National Convention in Atlantic City, they had been turned away—in spite of the universal knowledge that their opponents rested on cushions of violence and unconstitutional disenfranchisement. Now they had finally reached Washington with some thirty thousand pages of sworn depositions attesting the terror that had kept Negro Mississippians "apathetic" enough not to be voting. As if that weren't enough, they had ninety thousand "Freedom Ballots" cast in the face of a massive Ku Klux Klan and White Citizens Council campaign of intimidation, economic pressure and eviction. Representatives of the FDP had come to ask for the unseating of the white segregationists and for the calling of new elections in which all could participate—hardly a revolutionary goal in terms of the U. S. Constitution and the House Rules, which expressly provide for such a process.

The day we arrived it was about 110 degrees and we sat in St. Cyprian's, a Negro Catholic ghetto church not far from the Capitol, fanning ourselves with mimeographed handouts. Some chronicled the history of the FDP campaign and the voting records of the challenged congressmen, while others cried in outrage at the recent Johnson appointment of James Pleman Coleman, former governor of Mississippi and architect of the "Mississippi Plan" for legal disenfranchisement of Negroes, to the Federal Circuit Court in the South. (Washington, D.C., by the way, is perhaps the supreme ironic commentary on the War on Poverty, for it is one vast Negro ghetto with "pockets of luxury" dotted here and there—the White House, the Capitol, the various memorials, and the endless military cemeteries.) St. Cyprian's recreation room was filled with students, mostly white, and mostly from New York and the Bay Area, and an atmosphere of noisy apprehension hung in the air that was nearly wet enough to drink. The back of the hall was ringed with Student Nonviolent Coordinating Committee (SNCC) staff members up from Mississippi for the Challenge. Their names read like modern-day knights of the Round Table—Ivanhoe Donaldson, Courtland Cox, Ralph Featherstone—and they mostly lounged in knots of two or three, clad in Levis or overalls, discussing whatever gets discussed when guerrilla fighters leave a police state. One of them came forward to announce that Mrs. Victoria Gray, a would-be FDP Congressional candidate, would speak.

From the back of the room rose a tall, handsome Negro woman with skin the color of clear coffee, wearing a crisp white dress. The room fell silent as she began to speak, apologizing for not having a prepared talk. "There is a myth," she began, "that Negroes in Mississippi are apathetic, that they simply don't care about the poverty and indignity of their lives. That myth goes on to say that if Negroes in my state cared to remedy these things, they would have organized to do so long ago. . . ." There wasn't a trace of Southern accent in her voice, which reached the back of the room easily without a microphone. "What that myth ignores," she continued, "is the simple fact that Mississippi is, and has been for ninety years, a police state. I know, because in past years my neighbors and myself were completely unable to meet together and talk about ways of improving conditions without the threat of losing at the least our jobs and at the most our lives. Then, in 1960, came a group called the Student Nonviolent Coordinating Committee, a small number of young people, who began to help provide us with the one thing that was absolutely essential and that had formerly been unattainable: the ability to communicate—with each other, and from county to county." From the white students there were cheers and shouts of "Hear, Hear," but the SNCC staff members, who boast only of the victories of "local people," were silent.

"The organization that started when SNCC workers first came into Mississippi," Mrs. Gray went on, "has culminated in the Freedom Democratic party, a statewide organization open to anyone. Unlike the State Democratic party, this organization supports the national platform of the Democratic party, and in a Freedom election held last November, it polled more votes for Johnson than he received in the "legitimate" elections at the same time. . . . In Mississippi we say that the Freedom elections are real and the state elections are mock, because they are a mockery. . . ." At this there was applause and laughter.

"But it has only been since we came to Washington," the lady resumed, "that we have begun to realize how much bigger and broader this fight is than we ever thought. It is only since we've met with the pitiful rationalizations and excuses of congressmen and other Northern politicians, only since it's become quite clear that the word has come down from the *top* to defeat the Challenge, that we've finally understood the frightening truth that segregation and discrimination are not Mississippi throwbacks, but American institutions." Mrs. Gray had spent the weekend in jail for sitting-in at the office of the House Clerk who, obviously under orders from the Speaker and ultimately the President, had refused even to print the thirty thousand pages of sworn depositions of testimony taken the previous winter in Mississippi by Northern lawyers. Her voice rose now in a crescendo. "And it has been with the development of the Freedom Democratic party and this Challenge that people from all over the country have had the chance to support a movement which was a significant departure from the former pattern of an immediate crisis, a call for aid, perhaps the sending of some old clothes, canned food and a few dollars, and then going blithely on thinking everything was all right. The FDP and the Challenge mark the beginning for us of the realization that, while all are not guilty, all are responsible . . . and that until this struggle, and others like it, are won, we will not have begun to talk about democracy in this country."

Amid the shower of applause that followed as she sat down, the person I was with scibbled on my notes, "The first woman President of the United States will be black." I could only smile and agree.

I hardly need to record that the Challenge was resoundingly defeated when it finally came to the Floor in early fall. This only meant that those people went back to Mississippi, wiser and more knowledgeable about the opposition, to organize for next time. Of all the people I had a chance to observe at that time, including Senator

Eastland and the Southern-dominated Judiciary Committee, the person who made me sickest at heart was a well-known liberal democratic Congressman from California for whom I admit I had once even walked precincts. Perhaps the high point of our "briefing session" in his office occurred when a girl who'd spent several months with SNCC in Mississippi asked whether or not there would be a significant change in federal enforcement of the new Voting Bill, on which he had been expounding in glorious tones. "You know as well as I do," she said in a friendly way, "that the 1957, 1960 and 1964 Civil Rights Acts simply never beached in Mississippi." Looking dramatically and directly at her, he responded with the incredible question, "Young lady, are you a lawyer?" (The girl looked no more than twenty.) She answered, "No." "Well, then," he replied, "I'd prefer to discuss that with a lawyer."

The prevention of Negro Americans and others from fully participating in the rights and privileges of our country is the most immediate wrong against which protests are currently being directed. But there is also a discontent that is more of a deep, hollow fear, a poverty that cannot be measured in dollars. For what about that larger group of young people who have not been disinherited, those for whom the grateful acceptance of a split-level ranch-style existence is the "logical," the expected step? What about me, for example, and thousands of other students like me? I am twenty-three years old, of what the sociologists would call upper middle-class background; I hold a B.A. degree in political science, love to write, and possess practical skills that would enable me to get a well-paying job in any number of fields. What leads me to spend part of my summer combing the halls of Congress on behalf of the Mississippi Freedom Democratic Party, or most of my Christmas vacation picketing on the docks of Oakland to prevent the loading of grapes picked by non-union labor? Why should I care about the first major farm labor strike in California agribusiness since the 1930s? Why all of this when, as my mother yearly points out to me, I could be driving a nice car, making a "respectable" living, and raising a family?

At the center, for me, there is a great restlessness, a great longing to reach beyond the formica and gleaming stainless steel and to be able to touch other human beings. I want to be able to share with others the awe of a redwood tree and its inviolability in comparison to a highway; I want to do so without being considered a "nut," and with the satisfaction of feeling that my society also respects those values and will act accordingly. I want to be free from the compulsion to possess things and people, and to know that others are similarly free. I want to be able to love life enough to value it over all else, and to live in a society that shares that value. I want to feel that my own hands shape my life, free from the invisible strings of individual and social repression, and to know that others share that ability. I want to see no want in the midst of plenty. I want to know that our world will not be blown to bits in the name of any abstract principle, or for any other reason, by the hands of man. These things form the innermost core and are the hardest to talk about without sounding maudlin. But I am saying them anyway, because they do lie at the center and they are important to me. In short, I want to live in a society and a world that solves the problems that are tied around our necks like dead weights from the past—the problems of developing a more mature handling of sex, of overcoming poverty, of implementing basic human rights, and of achieving and keeping global peace. I want to live in a world that is able to get on to the questions that really belong to the twentieth century: What is the meaning of work? What is the fullest meaning of being human? What does it mean to love?

Our search for answers to these frontier questions appear to me inextricably bound up with the solutions we find for the most crying practical problems we today confront. For how, without raising the question of our notion of humanity, do I seek to understand a war in which, under the banner of self-determination and democracy, my country invades a foreign land, interferes in a civil war, sets up puppet governments, bombs hospitals, schools and whole villages of people who have never heard of democracy, burns children with jellied gasoline, and refuses to hold promised elections? How shall I comprehend "arming for peace" and living in a balance of terror? How shall I interpret the fact that "successful" executives often end up in the Mayo Clinic having their stomachs removed piece by piece for a nervous ulcer? Now that there is a chicken in almost every pot, and the pot is electric, and there are two or three cars in most garages, how do I explain or justify the one-fourth of our people who, even according to the most conservative estimates, do not approach sharing these things? How shall I reconcile Thomas Jefferson's words on revolution with our actions in the Dominican Republic? Can I really tell my children when they ask me about the murders of Viola Liuzzo, Michael Schwerner or Reverend Reeb that the killers never came to justice because under federal law it did not become a violation of a person's civil rights to murder him until the spring of 1966?

To be honest, I don't know how many Americans, or how many American students, share my concern with these questions. But there must be a good many. When magazines like *Esquire, Atlantic Monthly* and even *Mademoiselle* devote lead articles and whole issues to campus ferment, they must be reacting to something. Whatever position one cares to take on the free speech movement at the University of California in Berkeley, I daresay few people in the country were unaware that things were stirring there in a major way.

I am, however, much more sure of an underlying restlessness and feeling of dissatisfaction. All you really need to do to get a sense of it is to look at the almost incredible nationwide popularity of what jazz critic Ralph J. Gleason has called "one thin phenomenal youth"—Bob Dylan. Gleason claims on the best estimates that Dylan's royalties for the first six months of 1965 will be "greater than the combined royalties of Rodgers, Hart, Hammerstein, Gershwin and Porter for the same period."[1] On his tours, nearly all his concerts are sold out in advance, and not just in New York and Berkeley but all across the country. According to Gleason, he has published 225 songs, many of which have subsequently been recorded by other performers and a good number of which have been hits. What, then, is he saying that young people are listening to? Where is he hitting home?

I well remember my own first reaction to a Dylan concert. The auditorium was packed—mostly, it seemed, with young teen-agers. The entire audience, including myself, sat almost absolutely rapt for the whole performance. No screaming, no hysteria. During the intermission many people just wandered alone about the hallways staring

[1] Ralph J. Gleason, "This World" section of the *San Francisco Chronicle,* November 28, 1965, p. 35.

at the floor, as if what was coming through was so true, or painful, that to stand bantering and smoking over it would weaken or distort it. The next morning I wrote a letter to Gleason in which I said, for want of a better way to put it, "I don't know whether Dylan is the voice of my generation, but I do know that he is my voice."

Of course, Dylan's songs nowadays are all his own, and I think he is a poet even before he is a musician. There has also been a definite shift in style and lyrics, especially in the past several months. At the risk of tearing apart the petals of a flower just to find out what they're made of, I'd like to quote verses from some of the more popular songs, to help give an over-all indication of what Bob Dylan has been saying and of what we are listening to.

From the early "Blowin' in the Wind":

How many times must a man look up before he can see the sky?
Yes, 'n How many ears must one man have before he can hear people cry?
Yes, 'n How many deaths will it take till he knows that too many people
have died?
The answer, my friend, is blowin' in the wind,
The answer is blowin' in the wind.[2]

From another fairly early song, "With God on Our Side":

I've learned to hate Russians
All through my whole life
If another war starts
It's them we must fight.
To hate them and fear them,
To run and to hide,
And accept it all bravely
With God on my side.[3]

Also from a relatively early song:

Come Senators, Congressmen
Please heed the call
Don't stand in the doorway

[2] "Blowin' in the Wind." Copyright 1962 by M. Witmark & Sons. Used by permission.

[3] "With God on Our Side." Copyright 1963 by M. Witmark & Sons. Used by permission.

Don't block up the hall.
For he who gets hurt
Will be he who has stalled
There's a battle
Outside and it's ragin'
It'll soon shake your windows
And rattle your walls
For the times they are a-changin'![4]

From his record "Bringing It All Back Home," the song "Mr. Tambourine Man":

Then take me disappearin' through the smoke rings of my mind
Down the foggy ruins of time far past the frozen leaves
The haunted, frightened trees out to the windy beach
Far from the twisted reach of crazy sorrow
Yes, to dance beneath the diamond sky with one hand wavin' free
Silhouetted by the sea, circled by the circus sands
With all memory and fate driven deep beneath the waves
Let me forget about today until tomorrow.[5]

And finally, what I consider one of the most telling and beautiful stanzas from any of Dylan's songs, the ending of "It's All Right, Ma (I'm Only Bleedin')":

Although the masters make the rules
Of the wise men and the fools
I got nothing, Ma,
To live up to.[6]

There is one more record, "Highway 61 Revisited" in which the beat is very hard and swinging, and in which the imagery of "Gates of Eden" and "Mr. Tambourine Man" is carried even further, often into personal meanings that probably escape the listener. The trend is

4 "The Times They Are A-Changin'." Copyright 1963 (Unp) by M. Witmark & Sons in the U.S.A. Copyright 1964 by M. Witmark & Sons under the Universal Copyright Convention. Used by permission.

5 "Mr. Tambourine Man." Copyright 1964 (Unp) by M. Witmark & Sons in the U.S.A. Copyright 1965 by M. Witmark & Sons under the Universal Copyright Convention. Used by permission.

6 "It's All Right Ma (I'm Only Bleedin')." Copyright 1965 by M. Witmark & Sons. Used by permission.

away from the simple ballad with a clear message. As Dylan said in a San Francisco press conference, he had simply gone as far as he wanted to go with the early-type songs. That doesn't mean they're no longer valid; it's just that he's said those things and now wants to go on to others.

Critics have tried to show anomalous splits in his works, saying that he has three kinds of songs, the social-consciousness songs, the personal-introspective songs, and what they (but not he) call "folk-rock." I just don't think the breakdown is necessary or meaningful, at least if it is intended to imply some sort of inconsistency or dishonesty. For me there is an authentic relationship between Dylan's various songs and moods. It is a relationship that springs from a whole person who is striving to live meaningfully in America in this time—to love in spite of fear and alienation, to condemn the hidden executioners, persuaders and influencers, to prophesy major changes, and to search deeply inside himself for the wellsprings of joy and despair. Judging from the response of young people all over the United States, there must be many who share some of his longing and hope—even though they may not consciously comprehend the full impact of his words. This thin youth with three harmonicas, a guitar and a heart full of poetry has obviously tapped a great common well of discontent, frustration and yearning. Pete Seeger and Woody Guthrie tried to get out messages in many ways similar for years, but they never attained Dylan's phenomenal popularity, except among radicals already committed to the ideas.

I am reminded of the magnificent lines in W. H. Auden's poem "In Memory of W. B. Yeats":

> For poetry makes nothing happen: it survives
> In the valley of its saying where executives
> Would never want to tamper; it flows south
> From ranches of isolation and the busy griefs,
> Raw towns that we believe and die in; it survives,
> A way of happening, a mouth.[7]

The Dylan mouth is sometimes a whisper, sometimes a shout, sometimes a thin wail, sometimes a lyric melody that is in each way

[7] Copyright 1940 by W. H. Auden. Reprinted from *Another Time,* by W. H. Auden, by permission of Random House, Inc.

saying for millions of young people something central to the way they feel, not only with a sense of imagery and turns of phrase they couldn't write but, I submit, in most cases with ideas that have had to be buried stillborn in the unconscious because of the necessity of living and integrating into this society. Somehow, through the magic of an artistic experience, he is breaking through at an emotional level and, in a sense, reaching people from inside themselves.

While Bob Dylan thus appears to me the most gifted representative of youthful discontent with our present way of life, Erich Fromm offers what I believe are some of the most valuable clues to why so many Americans remain as encapsulated in the inconsistencies of our culture as they do. In *Beyond the Chains of Illusion*[8] Fromm attempts to sum up a lifetime of study inspired primarily by the writings of Marx and Freud. For me this book has gone a long way toward explaining the seeming paradox of how people can listen without really hearing, and feel without acting.

Fromm believes that, taken together, the works of Marx and Freud show us how human ideas and behavior are the products of two simultaneous forces: on the one hand, our deep-rooted, individual psychic needs and, on the other, the universal necessity of society to perpetuate itself. According to Marx, the ideas and behavior patterns that facilitate the economic and power relationships of a period soon assume the proportions of a social conscious, an ideology in terms of which human beings then come to understand and order their lives. Freud, for his part, has contributed the well-known notion of the individual unconscious. He developed this concept from his clinical discoveries that individuals repress their most important formative childhood experiences and that this leads to the result that "most of what is real within ourselves is not conscious, and most of what is conscious is not real."[9]

Fromm has combined Marx's and Freud's central insights and further developed them into the concept of the social unconscious. In effect, he suggests that Marx's social conscious needs to be viewed as having also an unconscious dimension. And he proposes that Freud's

[8] Erich Fromm, *Beyond the Chains of Illusion,* New York, Giant Cardinal Edition, Pocket Books, 1965.

[9] *Ibid.,* p. 96.

phenomenon of the unconscious is an aspect not only of the life of individuals but of society at large. It is because of the workings of this social unconscious that, in Fromm's words, "we repress also the awareness of facts, provided they contradict certain ideas and institutions which we do not want to have threatened."[10] The social unconscious in the case of a society, like the unconscious in the case of an individual, thus consists of what we consider vital to the continuance of our whole mode of living. And it follows that we guard it from threats just as jealously as we guard the deep emotional significance of early relationships with our parents and siblings. Thus, by the use of certain kinds of logic, by the unconscious repression of those facts which "don't fit" with our belief structures, and by the way we use language, it is possible to "filter out" those frightening, disturbing ideas or events which might challenge our values and life patterns. As Fromm puts it, "In order to convince himself that he acts according to his own free will, man invents rationalizations to make it appear as if he does what he does because he has to for moral or rational reasons."[11]

The clear implication is that when the filters are pervasive or effective enough, simple intellectual knowledge will not work. Like the person who gets drunk and forgets everything beyond the point at which he began to make a fool of himself, we can ignore or become insensitive to whatever does not jibe with our total psychological and social needs. This means, for Fromm, that change cannot come merely through understanding our experiences in theoretical or empirical terms; what is required is some sort of more basic emotional confrontation. Meanwhile, men have created, and lived in accordance with rules and justifications for behavior which Fromm collectively calls "illusions." That realization leads him to what I consider the core of the book: "We are determined by forces outside our conscious selves, and by passions and interests which direct us behind our backs. Inasmuch as this is the case, we are not free. But we can emerge from this bondage and enlarge the realm of freedom by becoming fully aware of reality, and hence, of necessity, by giving up illusions and transforming ourselves from somnambulistic, unfree,

[10] *Ibid.*, p. 106.
[11] *Ibid.*, p. 108.

determined, defensive, passive persons into awakened, aware, active, independent ones."[12]

Such a recognition is very important. For without realizing that built-in, unconscious societal forces can and do deaden sensitivity, it is impossible to understand not only Hitler's Germany, but a nation that can read daily—now even on the front pages of its newspapers—about the tragic and pointless deaths of children and civilians as well as "the enemy" at the hands of our troops, and not begin to question the war in Vietnam. The press has become so outraged at restrictions placed on news coverage that I believe in many cases Americans are getting an accurate picture of the war and its contradictions, as well as of the absurd degree to which news management is being carried. But President Johnson waves a fatherly hand and drawls out the tired, trite clichés about democracy and freedom, and the polls show that the vast majority agrees with his conduct of foreign policy in Southeast Asia. He sends out "peace feelers" to Delhi and Toronto but few question why not to Hanoi or National Liberation Front Headquarters in South Vietnam. Few wonder at the contradiction between our talk of "self-determination" and the reports droned out by television commentators showing that American military installations in Vietnam are being designed on a thirty-year timetable. One or two letters to the editor are the response to a photograph on the front page of the *San Francisco Chronicle* which shows a "Viet Cong" body draped over the hood of a jeep like a deer bagged by happy hunters in the Sierras.

The same is true of other kinds of atrocities to which Americans seem on the whole quite comfortably accommodated. In 1964 in Mississippi, when the FBI and National Guard were combing the Pearl River for the bodies of the three slain civil rights workers, two other bodies were dredged up. At first there was a furor because it was thought those were the corpses of two of the missing three. When it was learned they were not, the whole question was dropped. No one seemed overly concerned. I asked in Washington in the summer of 1965 whose bodies they had been, and was told by SNCC staff people that they were "just a couple of niggers from a nearby Negro college. . . ." No publicity, no questions, no fanfare, from the South

[12] *Ibid.*, p. 118.

or from the North, even though there was front-page coverage across the nation.

I think the easiest way to explain such things is that the defense mechanisms of people's social unconscious are operating to keep their capacities for awareness and sensitivity inhibited. The transformation Fromm talks of, from the condition of forgetfulness and emotional numbness to one of being aware, active and independent is extremely important. For it represents a process essential to overcoming slavery to social and psychological illusions that blind and deafen us. But where I think Fromm falls short is in his failure to explain how such a transformation can be achieved. Let us return for a moment to Bob Dylan. Surely to him we can apply all those criteria of one who is liberated from the prevailing illusions and who can write and sing about them, sometimes tearing away so many layers of himself that he gets into completely personal imagery which can only be enjoyed like some of Dylan Thomas' poetry, as cadence and rhythm and individually forged word usage. Many people listen to him, and for a great many of them his music is emotionally stimulating; yet only a small proportion probably truly change as a result. It seems to me that if all those who bought his records and attended his concerts reacted to the content of his songs, there would surely be many more people in the civil rights and peace movements, or at least more who in other ways were saying "No" to the banal conformity of American society today. It may be that for some, listening to him is a sort of "secret life of Walter Mitty." Or perhaps they are touched only enough to be troubled. But in any case, these reactions are not enough to make for major changes in behavior, even though they do set the stage.

Fromm propounds a basic humanistic credo according to which man holds the power of affirmation or negation, the power to choose individually or in concert, life patterns that will enhance or degrade the quality of human existence. He says that "man's task in life is precisely the paradoxical one of realizing his individuality and transcending it in arriving at the experience of universality . . . and all one can do for another is to show him the alternatives, truthfully and lovingly yet without sentimentality or illusion."[13]

[13] *Ibid.*

I believe that this is true on a person-to-person level. But I also think that Fromm avoided his own dilemma regarding the filters which are so crucial a factor in keeping most people from being able to hear and act on sets of alternatives that transcend their current value orientations. It seems to me romantically to avoid the central and practical problem of how to reach large numbers of people. And if you want to go beyond scattered individual instances of awareness spread ineffectively throughout a population, you simply must be concerned about reaching large numbers of people.

In talking to one of the activities counselors here at San Francisco State College, I learned that in 1966 more freshmen than ever before had asked during the orientation period about extracurricular programs that would deal with the problems of war and peace and civil rights, or that would put them in touch with other students on a large, impersonal-appearing campus. I don't pretend to know all the reasons for this. Perhaps they were only curious. Perhaps they were afraid of being drafted. Perhaps they were reacting to Dylan and others in the field of entertainment. Or it may be that they had just accumulated enough of a burden of loneliness, dissatisfaction and alienation to feel that they had to deal with it someway. At any rate, they had somehow come to the door that questions the prevalent illusions, and it was likely that a budding awareness would develop, one way or another. It seems to me that it is up to us older students who are interested in breaking down those illusions to help them respond to these needs for answers and for contact with other people. We must face up to these needs in a meaningful way. We must make possible experiences which will combine some sort of person-to-person relationship with understanding of the problems and alternatives that they confront in their own immediate environment, the problems and alternatives of action or submission, of mere rejection or creative challenge. For the fact is that the dilemma of alienation and awareness can be handled in many ways. It can be met by some form of escape—by physically and/or psychologically "unplugging" oneself from the society. One can, for example, take the way of the "beatnik" and settle for only negative values. Or as some friends of mine have done, one can move to an isolated farm where, in effect, a different existence is created and one practically ceases to communicate with the world at large. Another way the dilemma can be met is by searching deeper and deeper within one's own self and coming up with some kind of personally creative response (such as art or writing) or else indulging in drugs or other experiences that set up a "world within the world"; this in a sense affords a manner of coexistence with society, but no real participation. And the third major alternative is to begin to look at one's environment with a willingness seriously to question it and its precepts, to work to change it, and to seek to break down its illusions and masked injustices—not in terms of any unquestioned ideology or plan, but with a constant readiness to integrate new information and experiences and to try to incorporate them as part of one's own guidelines. This path also means taking responsibility for the bright and damning light such an approach can shed on the system in which we live.

I opt for that third alternative, which I should like to call creative challenge. That does not mean, of course, that I recommend excluding all parts of the others. (I myself, for example, am working in creative writing and also try my hand at various art forms.) It does mean a basic commitment to acting for the implementation of changes we see as necessary, rather than just accepting the fact that the world is full of things we do not like and feeling that there is no point in trying to do anything about it. But if one really wants to be effective, to make significant changes, and not simply to satisfy oneself psychologically, opting for creative challenge means much more than a simple yes-or-no commitment. Above all, it means avoiding the temptation to exchange one set of illusions for another. I believe that ultimately the challenge lies in developing a new style which will transcend the no-content dialogue of two-party politics in the United States as well as the isolation and ineffectiveness of most radical groups, which usually wind up talking to other radical groups or to small bands of their own faithful. Very often, in fact, radical groups actually fear contact that will mean real chances for effecting change. They do so either because the members have become so alienated that they are incapable of talking and relating to outsiders, or because their goals are not real in other than ideological terms and they wouldn't know how to institute them even if they had the opportunity.

One of the most important ways of working for change that avoid these pitfalls is to start within the student's own environment, at the college itself. Indeed, all over the country students are questioning not only restrictions on speech and activity, but content and approach in the classroom and the curriculum. They are beginning to ask how much of what is being taught is truly relevant to their experiences and needs and to the problems they believe need solving. And they are beginning to look for ways in which they themselves can supplement the existing curriculum with courses and programs of their own. These innovations are of an experimental nature, and may or may not one day find their way into the regular academic offerings. They are open to criticism and revision, able to grow with the needs and curiosities of the participants. And they are very much in the spirit of creative challenge. Their purpose is critically to compare what students see around them with the concepts they are taught in the classroom to see where the discrepancies lie, to root out possible academic illusions and expose them to the light of question.

Such things are happening today at San Francisco State College under the auspices of the Associated Students. Student government over the last three or four years has evolved a basic philosophy which recognizes that the college will be the student's community for about four years and which assumes that to the extent he actively questions at every step, avoids being just a passive vessel into which "knowledge" is poured, and seeks interpersonal relationships with teachers and fellow students, he will be contributing both to his own development and the bettering of the school. To that end, we have sought and won seats for students on all major college policy-making boards, including every commiteee of the Academic Senate. Students are working on the development of a body of curriculum criticism and evaluation that will hopefully make an important contribution to program changes and innovations in shared classroom experiences for faculty and students.

One semester we decided to start open-ended discussion groups with freshmen and sophomores to mull over anything they felt to be of interest, anything that troubled them about their education, their lives, and what it meant to be eighteen and in college in 1965. Out of these groups emerged what we now call "the GEEP," or General

Educational Experimental Program. Nearly twenty of those freshmen and sophomores had not been satisfied with just talking and griping. So they set out to design and organize their own general education program, recruiting professors from the faculty and breaking down artificial departmental barriers marked "specialization."

Associated Students funds are also bringing to the campus visiting professors such as Paul Goodman. His biting criticism of education and the Academy (not to mention society at large) may keynote a spring which has already brought to fruition what we call "the Special Section," or "the Experimental College." This experimental college within the college was in many ways the next logical step beyond mere criticism of the system. For it is an attempt to try our own hand at organizing seminars, classes, and series of talks and lectures for the purpose of supplementing and, we hope, cross-fertilizing, the regular curriculum. In our first semester over twenty courses were offered, most of which had optional academic credit available. The areas of exploration ranged from nonviolence to avant-garde philosophy, from group process and community organization to critical thinking. In fact, I even organized one seminar called "Something Big: Art and the Campus Environment," in which we tried to bring creativity, art and functional design to bear on our own college community. Specifically, by working together we may find ways of imbuing the college's "neo-penal" architecture with somewhat more human proportions.

Well over three hundred students are now involved in "the Special Section," and interest is growing at least as fast as we can meet it. The whole experiment is permeated by a feeling, a mood—ever so difficult to touch or define, but somehow very much in the air. It is a mood of community and affirmation, an unwritten, between-the-lines kind of sense that somehow emerges from chaos. I guess what it says is that we can do it, that we are doing it—exploring what that means as we go, often groping awkwardly, but nonetheless *doing it.* You seldom hear anyone talk in stereotyped ways about *"the"* Administration (as though it were an iron bastion without people who can listen, understand and be enthused). For the cooperation we've found among administrators and faculty alike has been little short of amazing and certainly wouldn't validate anyone's stereotypes. In fact, many of these people appear to feel they have as big a stake in our growth and success as we do ourselves.

The other major assumption of student government here at San Francisco State is that the college is not an isolated cloister but is unavoidably (and thankfully) a part of the community outside. It affects, and is affected by, the larger community—whether consciously or unconsciously. The college—this one or any other—is a great resource of knowledge and trained people. But college students also have much to learn by mixing experiences in the world outside with academic knowledge gained from their books and classrooms. Many times practical experience gained in community work can have far-reaching results by way of revising theories long cherished but no longer workable. I would cite as an example the contribution to both the community and the college that has been made by San Francisco State's Tutorial Program, an operation involving four hundred student tutors with as many grade-school and high-school tutees from areas of poverty and cultural deprivation. On the one hand, many of the preconceptions with which these students entered such areas as San Francisco's Fillmore and Mission districts have altered drastically. On the other hand, representatives of the Tutorial Program are suggesting sweeping changes in the educational curriculum in areas that bear on their experiences.

It is our ardent hope that the Tutorial Program is just the first in a series of undertakings from which will grow a creative interchange between San Francisco State and the community around it. With this in mind, we have this semester initiated the "Community Involvement Program," which is beginning to involve students in a broad range of community projects, including the development of a model integrated community to the southeast of the College, a Student Union in the city's Haight-Ashbury District, and the provision of pickets and fund-raising in support of striking Delano grape pickers.

I think there is one underlying principle that knits all these activities together. Perhaps creative challenge is a good term, perhaps not; but the crux of it is that students are bringing themselves to bear—and helping to bring others to bear—on their actual, living environment. They are working at the examination and eventual replacement of institutionalized illusions that make us less human, more prone to destructiveness and less creative. In all these ways students are saying no to all forms of passive submissiveness, demanding an active role in the shaping of their destinies, and showing a willingness to help others do the same. After all, students in Students for a Democratic Society in Newark, New Jersey, with their motto "Let the people decide," and students in Mississippi, developing indigenous community leadership to fight a century-old struggle, are really making the same discovery that we are making on the campus. We have all discovered that apathy is a word behind which the fearful hide. Apathy means not seeing the possibility of effecting change; it means having rejected the easy sham answers and having become cynical about them. But apathy can vanish, to be replaced by commitment, when people learn together the ways they can make a difference.

Format by Mort Perry
Set in 10/12 Linotype Times Roman
Composed, printed and bound by American Book–Stratford Press, Inc.
HARPER & ROW, PUBLISHERS, INCORPORATED

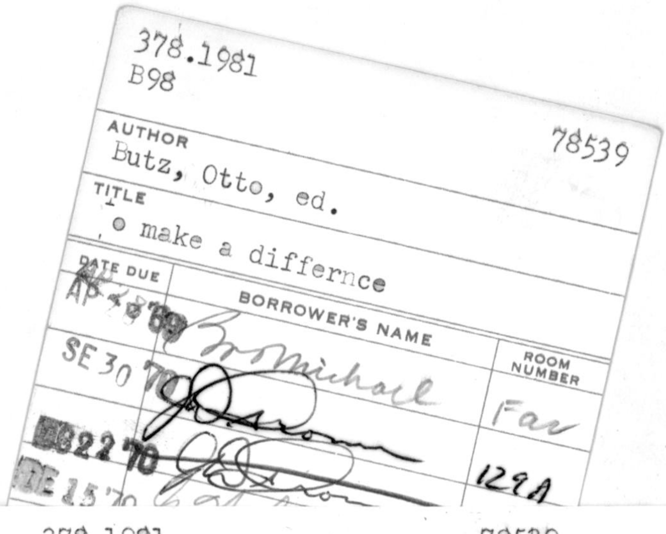

Date Due

AP 28 '69				
SE 30 '70				
OC 22 '70				
DE 15 '70				